TOTAL QUALITY MARKETING

TOTAL QUALITY MARKETING

The Key to Regaining Market Shares

Allan C. Reddy

Quorum Books

Westport, Connecticut • London

Library of Congress Cataloging-in-Publication Data

Reddy, Allan C.
    Total quality marketing : the key to regaining market shares /
Allan C. Reddy.
        p.   cm.
    Includes bibliographical references and index.
    ISBN 0–89930–893–7 (alk. paper)
    1. Marketing–United States–Quality control. 2. Total quality
management–United States. I. Title.
    HF5415.1.R415 1994
    658.8′02–dc20   94–15885

British Library Cataloguing in Publication Data is available.

Library of Congress Catalog Card Number: 94–15885
ISBN: 0–89930–893–7

First published in 1994

Quorum Books, 88 Post Road West, Westport, CT 06881
An imprint of Greenwood Publishing Group, Inc.

Printed in the United States of America

The paper used in this book complies with the
Permanent Paper Standard issued by the National
Information Standards Organization (Z39.48–1984).

10 9 8 7 6 5 4 3 2 1

To Valdosta State University,
a high-quality educational institution
in southeast Georgia

Contents

Tables and Figures

TABLES

FIGURES

Preface

Today, American managers are in a dilemma. They are overwhelmed by foreign competition in every business—from cars to cameras. How to beat and contain formidable competitors from Japan, Germany, and other countries whose appetite for devouring market shares is endless? How to regain market shares? These questions need prompt answers. This book is about how American firms can regain market shares by using Total Quality Marketing (TQMkt). TQMkt is an advanced version of the "Four Ps" model in marketing.

At present, many firms are embracing Total Quality Management (TQM) as if it were a panacea. However, in today's dynamic global business environment, success depends equally on applying Total Quality Marketing (TQMkt). Unless customers perceive quality improvements properly, improving product quality alone is insufficient to propel a product to success in the marketplace. A good example is the lagging sales of American-made automobiles despite significant quality improvements in these cars made by the Big Three U.S. automakers. Car buyers continue to perceive that imports are better.

TQM is a buzzword in modern business circles. Some American managers are blindly pursuing it while ignoring the quality aspects of the marketing strategy. Meanwhile, foreign competitors are moving a step ahead. Having fulfilled manufacturing quality standards, many foreign firms are busy improving their marketing quality, an action that will only further widen the gap with their U.S. competitors.

By putting profits into more advanced manufacturing and management technologies, foreign competitors are becoming even more formidable. Each year competitors from Japan, Germany, and Southeast Asia seem to grow stronger than ever. They constantly introduce better-quality products, increasing their global market shares.

For example, Japan and Southeast Asian countries took advantage of their low wages to penetrate deep into the lucrative and fertile U.S. and Western markets. They built huge fortunes in the process. Japan now is proclaimed as the number one economic power in the world. Japan could achieve this status by exporting high-quality, low-priced manufactured goods to the rich and open U.S. and Western markets. These markets have been receptive to imports because of high labor and social maintenance costs.

Foreign competitors have many more advantages. They operate in a less regulative environment. Most do not have complex laws that restrict mergers, nor do they have anticorrupt-practice laws like those of the United States, which inhibit overseas expansion of U.S. firms. In many developing countries where bribery and corruption are common practice, American firms are hindered. They are unable to compete for contracts and new businesses like their foreign counterparts.

Second, some foreign governments encourage overseas expansion of their domestic firms. These governments also restrict imports of manufactured goods, agricultural products, and services that may jeopardize the business of the local firms. The fact that these governments are signatories of General Agreement on Tariff and Trade (GATT) does not seem to stop them from doing so. Furthermore, imports are not enthusiastically marketed in these countries by local intermediaries. They use subtle and not-so-subtle barriers that include cultural biases, complex distribution structures, and exhortations to the public to buy locally manufactured goods only.

For example, Japanese firms are protected by their government from imports competing against them in the Japanese markets. Japan is notorious for many nontariff and unwritten trade policies that discourage foreign-made products from entering the Japanese markets. For example, despite serious efforts, American cigarette manufacturers are unable to penetrate the Japanese markets. In services such as insurance and banking, foreign businesses are very much restricted.

Unfortunately, there is no immediate solution to the foreign competition problem. Any drastic remedy evokes controversy from influential special-interest groups. Also, the recommendations often reflect the ideological orientation of experts who make and support such recommendations. For instance, proponents of free trade and exporting nations prefer the status quo. On the other hand, domestic manufacturers and labor unions want tough measures against imports.

Some experts suggest extreme measures such as managed competition as a remedy (Waldman 1986). Under managed competition, a government carefully evaluates the pros and cons of allowing imports freely. It watches over the imports with an intent to protect the interests of domestic industry and labor and then regulates the activities of foreign competitors accordingly.

The book has eight chapters. Chapter 1 presents the problem of loss of market shares. Chapter 2 evaluates imports to identify major competitors and what they export to the United States. It also discusses the implications of losing market shares. Chapter 3 focuses on the SWOT analysis. It evaluates the strengths, weaknesses, opportunities, and threats of U.S. versus foreign firms. Chapter 4 explains the market share mystique. Chapter 5 introduces Total Quality Marketing, the main concept, along with other concepts like Market Perceived Quality (MPQ) and Just Noticeable Difference (JND). Chapter 6 explains how Total Quality Marketing is currently implemented in some firms. Also, the scope for using TQMkt in services marketing, retailing, and direct marketing is discussed. Chapter 7 shows the integration of quality into marketing through company examples. Finally, Chapter 8 provides a concluding commentary by looking into the future. Information indirectly related to the topic is placed in the appendixes. The book has a readings list to supplement the extensive list of references.

Acknowledgments

The author gratefully acknowledges the editorial review and helpful suggestions of the following individuals: Mr. Eric Valentine, publisher of Quorum Books; and Professors Bruce D. Buskirk, Wade Humphreys, Ajit Kaicker, Jim Muncy, C. P. Rao, and Niren M. Vyas. The author is also especially grateful to Miss Aparna Reddy for editing the manuscript.

TOTAL QUALITY
MARKETING

CHAPTER 1

The Problem:
Loss of Market Shares

American managers need to be alert to foreign competition from a different perspective. To protect themselves from further market share losses and to regain lost market shares, American firms need innovative marketing strategies in tune with the changing times of the 1990s. This introductory chapter deals with the unique aspects of the foreign competition problem and sets the stage for the remainder of the book.

In an age of information revolution, having the "information edge" over competition is important. Foreign firms have more information about U.S. businesses and the U.S. business environment than American firms have about foreign businesses and the foreign business environments.

By taking advantage of open markets, foreign competitors keep flooding U.S. markets with low-price high-quality manufactured products, thereby causing big market share losses to many U.S. firms. Large market share losses have been especially conspicuous in automobile, steel, textile, and machine tool industries (Kotler 1988, p. 33).

LOSS OF MARKET SHARES TO FOREIGN COMPETITORS

Since the early 1960s, foreign competitors from Japan and Southeast Asian countries have been flooding U.S. markets with their low-cost high-quality products, grabbing market shares of the U.S. firms at a fast pace. Between 1980 and 1986, import penetration increased from 26 to 34 percent in durable goods; from 4 to 12 percent in communications; from 3 to 29 percent in computer and office equipment; and from 9 to 21 percent in instruments (Weber 1988, p. 131).

Worldwide, U.S. industries lost 50 percent of the market share in a wide range of goods in such industries as automobiles, food processors, cameras, stereo equipment, medical equipment, color television sets, hand tools, radial tires, electric motors, microwave ovens, athletic equipment, computer chips, industrial robots, electronic microscopes, machine tools, and optical equipment (Godfrey and Kolesar 1988, pp. 213–238).

Foreign competition is not bad by any means. In democratic societies, competition of any kind is usually good. It helps protect citizens from exploitation by businesses. Coming from a variety of cultures, however, foreign competitors play business games by different rules from those followed by American firms. Therefore, to know and understand how these firms compete so successfully is extremely important for American firms, especially those that are in striking distance from foreign competitors in domestic or global markets.

Though some American-made products, like Levi's Jeans and California wines, are still popular worldwide, the list of successful American products is getting smaller each year as foreign competitors continue to grab market shares away from American firms, as in automobiles and other businesses. Today, videocassette recorders, photocopy machines, and television sets are no longer made in America. Nor are typewriters, now that Smith Corona has moved to Mexico.

Even some American cars, notably the Ford Festiva and Pontiac LeMans are made in South Korea; the Chevrolet Lumina and Plymouth Voyager in Canada; the Mercury Capri in Australia; and the Dodge Stealth in Japan.

According to Robert B. Reich (1990, pp. 53–64), about 30 to 40 percent of the imports come from U.S. firms operating from countries like Taiwan and South Korea. By shifting manufacturing overseas, the United States is losing the "economic multiplier" to other countries, a process that only made foreign MNCs (Mitsubishi, Samsung) richer, stronger, and more invincible. The foreign MNCs enrich the wealth of their own countries far more than that of the United States.

Misperceptions about the manufacturing origins of a product can sometimes create problems. One year, the city of Greece, New York, needed to purchase an earth-moving machine. Two parties submitted bids: a John Deere (an American company) and a Komatsu (a Japanese Company). The Komatsu machine cost $15,000 less than the John Deere, but the city leaders chose the latter because they wanted to be patriotic. It turned out that the John Deere machine was made in Japan while the Komatsu was made in the United States.

The United States once dominated global business, earning a reputation for "Coca-colonizing" the world. Today the world has been transformed to a "Toyota World," where consumers are inundated with a flood of Japanese products. How did it happen?

In forty years, Japan moved from a war-ravaged, poor nation to a very rich nation. Its citizens enjoyed a per capita income of $22,000 in 1992 while the per capita income in the United States for the same period was about $19,000. A macroeconomic behavior model explaining reasons for the Japanese economic miracle has been postulated (Reddy, Oliver, Rao, and Addington 1984). Internally, the Japanese people had three qualities: the right attitude, adaptation, and achievement motivation. Externally, the Japanese firms have been helped by a supportive government, cooperative labor unions, and unwaveringly diligent people. Finally, Japan's export push is matched by the import pull in Western countries that have been hungry for high-quality low-priced goods.

How did the United States lose its economic advantage? Soon after World War II, American firms enjoyed two major advantages that aided their rapid growth. First, it was easy to open businesses and succeed because of economic conditions created by war buildup. Second, firms that participated in government-sponsored reconstruction programs made huge profit bonanzas because there was little competition from other countries. Such favorable conditions lead to the rapid growth of many of today's American business monoliths like Coca-Cola and General Motors.

UNIQUE ASPECTS OF FOREIGN COMPETITORS

Foreign competitors have certain unique strengths that American firms need to be aware of. Globally dominant U.S. firms seriously underestimated the capabilities of aggressive competitors from Japan, West Germany, and other countries as they began to recover from the destruction of war. These competitors had a strong desire to succeed. Encouraged and supported by governments that were equally desperate to rebuild their war-torn economies, foreign competitors spared no efforts in rebuilding their industries. Using imported technology and modern marketing ideas, foreign competitors chipped away market shares from many U.S. firms.

Foreign competitors had an added advantage—the availability of abundant low-cost labor. Most of them started with labor-intensive low-technology industries. After gaining skills and strength, some competitors shifted to high-technology industries. The Japanese in particular had an abundance of skilled labor available at low cost. Thus, by the early 1970s, firms from Japan and West Germany had competed for and won market shares from American firms. Market share losses occurred in industries ranging from autos to cameras.

MAJOR CONCERNS

A major concern today is that foreign competition has grown so huge that its impact is felt in almost all industries. Efforts of some U.S. firms to restrain foreign competitors entering U.S. markets have been unsuccessful or produced negligible results. Market shares lost to foreign competitors have become extremely difficult to regain. This is especially true when consumers develop loyalty to foreign brands, and the foreign competitors become more adept in defending their turfs. Most foreign manufacturers have reinvested their profits into further improvement of their products and marketing efforts to improve their competitive positions. Thus, foreign competitors make it difficult for U.S. firms to recapture lost markets.

Another major concern is loss of jobs and loss of the economic multiplier effect. Technically, the multiplier effect relates to changes in the net national product (NNP) brought about by changes in total increases in income. A small change in the investment plans of business or the consumption savings plans of households can trigger a much larger change in equilibrium level of NNP. The multiplier magnifies the fluctuation in business activity initiated by changes in spending (McConnell and Brue 1990).

In 1993, the United States, Canada, and Mexico joined in the North American Free Trade Agreement (NAFTA). According to this agreement, the participating countries will have free access to each other's markets. Because of NAFTA, many American firms will move into Mexico to take advantage of low labor costs there. The prospect of losing jobs to Mexico made NAFTA unpopular with many Americans who resisted the agreement. The U.S. economy is already in recession. Unemployment is on the rise, and more companies are laying people off. In this environment, NAFTA is unwelcome to many Americans.

America's trade deficit is a major threat to the U.S. economy. Trade deficits are increasing rapidly, particularly with Japan, West Germany, and the Southeast Asian NICs (Newly Industrialized Countries) of Hong Kong, Singapore, South Korea, and Taiwan. The United States has developed large and chronic trade deficits with these countries in the last two decades. Even with some LDCs (Less Developed Countries) like Brazil and India, the United States is accumulating trade deficits. There is a potential threat from firms from other countries too as Eastern Europe, the former U.S.S.R., and China, as well as other countries, want to sell products in the lucrative American market.

According to Lester Thurow, America's trade deficit with Japan, Germany, and other nations is leading to a situation comparable to the black holes in outer space. Gravitational forces are so strong inside a black hole that not even light can get out—therefore the name. Since no one can devise a way to enter it, a black hole has to be deduced from what cannot be seen. The same situation prevails in our current structural trade imbalances. While trade deficits and surpluses have existed before, they have never been so large or existed for so long a time (Thurow 1993, p. 229).

Foreign competition is expanding into the service sector also. Banking, insurance, real estate, hotels, movies, restaurants and fast food, and construction are among the latest targets of foreign firms. Foreign banks with huge assets thrive in major U.S. cities. According to a *Fortune* report, Japanese banks hold 25 percent of California's banking assets, with a combined value of $93.4 billion, outweighing the Bank of America's $83 billion (Bylinsky 1989, p. 44). Glickman and Woodward (1989) maintain that the major reason for growing foreign investment in the United States is America's loss of international competitiveness.

According to Burton, the two important reasons for the trade deficit are heavy consumption of foreign goods and the inability of American firms to penetrate markets of other countries (1989, p. 13). This huge external debt creates a destabilizing effect on the already heavily debt-ridden economy and stifles its industrial growth and competitiveness. Loans lead to future interest payments that must be sent abroad. Both are subtractions from future U.S. living standards (Thurow 1993, p. 235).

Critics often point to Japan as a major offender. Because the United States has accumulated a trade deficit of one trillion dollars with that country, Japan gets the blame. Among major trading partners, Japan is the only one on war footing (Cohen 1985, p. 163). In spite of frequent Japan bashing, Japanese exports to the United States are not slowing. Instead, Japan now exports more expensive big-ticket items like luxury automobiles. Toyota's Lexus and Nissan's Infiniti are successfully competing in the Cadillac and Lincoln Continental market segments. Japan also dominates in the export of high-tech products like the latest computers, laser color printers, camcorders, and other items. Consequently, not only is Japan's trade gap with the United States widening, but the relationships between the two countries are becoming strained. Five years ago, Bruce Scott justifiably observed, "Increasingly, the United States to Japan is, say, as Brazil is to the United States—a commodity seller and a high-tech buyer" (1989, p. 116).

While foreign firms ravage U.S. markets with impunity, their home markets remain closed to American products and services through complex nontariff barriers and other restrictions. For example, despite outward assurances by Japan, its important industries—including construction—remain virtually closed to foreign companies. Moreover, Japan buys only limited quantities of rice, beef, citrus fruits, and cigarettes from the United States in order to protect its own agricultural and tobacco industries.

Two occurrences simultaneously benefit foreign competition. Foreign competitors are taking fullest advantage of America's economic and business problems, such as budget deficits, declining quality and productivity levels, and tolerant trade policies. Most American firms are facing problems that are endemic and structural; therefore, the trade deficit cannot be resolved in a short time. See Appendix A for a list of major economic issues.

In addition, the declining competitive spirit in American businesses strengthens the foreign competitors, making the threat more serious. Five years ago, McGrath found a disturbing trend of disillusionment among businesses: "No one listens anymore because nothing works. . . . Strategy has taken a back seat to execution" (McGrath 1988, p. xi). There is some evidence that American businesses are fighting back. Several companies are making necessary commitments and pursuing appropriate strategies to withstand foreign competitive attacks. Texas Instruments, NCR, 3M, Black and Decker, and Harley-Davidson are some good examples. This trend clearly shows that combating foreign competition and restoring American competitive strength can be viable business goals. To achieve these goals, critical strategic variables must be identified.

According to some marketing scholars (Kotler, Fahey, and Jatusripitak 1985, p. 243), U.S. firms have four options for defense and counterattack: (1) invite government protection and pressure on the foreign competitors, (2) encourage the government to seek joint ventures that would benefit both U.S. and foreign firms, (3) forge beneficial private cooperative arrangements with certain foreign firms, and (4) restructure the private competitive strategy to compete more effectively against rising new competition. Most U.S. firms use a mix of these response strategies, with emphasis changing over time. Most of all, the U.S. firms should develop new strategic thinking. Now more than ever, businesses need innovative strategic approaches that will deal with foreign competition in the twenty-first century.

THE NEED FOR INNOVATIVE STRATEGIES

Clearly, American firms should search for new strategies to solve problems. Strategic planning is not new to American business; it was first introduced in the mid-1950s (Steiner 1979, p. vii). However, new thinking and new direction are needed to successfully compete in today's dynamic environment. "The dogmas of the quiet past will not work in the turbulent future. As our cause is new, so must we think and act anew" (Abraham Lincoln, quoted in Ansoff 1988, p. xv).

Traditionally, strategic planning in U.S. firms focused on domestic competition more than on foreign competition. Till the 1970s, the U.S. market was completely dominated by American firms. Only since the 1980s has the severity of foreign competition in domestic markets become more obvious, as industry after industry fell to foreign competitors. To restore their competitiveness, U.S. firms must pursue new strategic directions. These strategies must include launching a full-scale marketing warfare against foreign competitors, first in domestic markets and then in foreign markets.

MARKETING WARFARE

Literature relating warfare to marketing has been growing fast (Michaelson 1987). According to Duro and Sandstrom (1987), Swedish marketing consultants, military thinking has often been associated with commercial marketing strategy, and it has always been applied in politics and business. Several writers assume that because there is little difference to separate modern politics from strategy and economics, one can apply military–strategic theories to marketing (Kotler and Sing 1981).

Duro and Sandstrom (1987, p. 1) point out that companies fail to deal with aggressive foreign competitors because they lack systematic strategies. Japanese companies, however, are well known for their deliberate strategies as they constantly keep introducing new products into various market segments. Firms lacking knowledge of basic tenets of strategy can easily fall prey to the Japanese offensive. Strategy-oriented companies invariably win in confrontations with strategically ignorant competitors.

In a highly fragmented marketing environment, a holistic perspective is necessary. Instead of trying to solve complex problems with simple solutions, individual firms should develop their own sets of strategies based on a better understanding of the macro and micro environments in which they operate. Philosophically, strategy is similar to a mass of water breaking violently through a dam:

The nature of water is that it avoids heights and hastens to the lowlands. When a dam is broken, the water cascades with irresistible force. Now the shape of an army resembles water. Take advantage of the enemy's unpreparedness; attack him when he does not expect it; avoid the strength and strike his emptiness, and like water, none can oppose you. Sun Tzu, 500 B.C. (quoted in Duro and Sandstrom, 1987, p. 2)

The basic ideas of marketing warfare are psychological—to find the opponents' weaknesses and pound on those weaknesses with the firm's distinctive competence until the competitors wear out. New approaches to strategic thinking include adopting modern marketing concepts like the "market perceived product quality," and "quality integrated marketing mix."

MESMERIZING CUSTOMERS BY OFFERING "VALUE"

The goal of any business must be to achieve customer satisfaction, the key to marketing success. What customers want is "value," that is, quality and reliability in a product at a reasonable price (Harrington 1987, p. 6). The starting point of traditional marketing strategy is identification of customers' needs and production of a product or service that fills specific needs of the customer groups or the market segments. It should be added that by providing Total Quality Marketing companies should aim to satisfy their target markets more effectively.

Today, we live in a world of "product inflation"—too many products chasing too few customers. When too many firms compete for the same target markets with identical products, traditional marketing approaches fail. To achieve success, then, a firm must clearly identify and thoroughly analyze its customers and its competitors. Strategies must be devised to satisfy customers while restraining competition before it strikes the firm's current or future target markets.

PREDICTING COMPETITOR STRATEGIES

Predicting competitor strategies and preparing countermoves is important. For example, consider the advance moves of Japanese firms in tapping the new U.S. markets. According to a *Fortune* magazine report,

Loaded with cash and eager to head off fire-breathing challenges from Korea and other growing Asian dragons, the folks who brought you the Walkman, the VCR, and the Honda are readying a sunburst of new products and services. Among them are tape recorders the size of a match box and flat TV screens that you can hang on walls. The Japanese will go after new business where they have only beachheads or no presence at all—even hamburgers in Honolulu. Rivals beware. (Bylinsky 1989, pp. 42–52)

Moreover, it is important to recognize that strategic thinking and knowledge are not limited to a few firms. Competitors also develop their own sets of counterstrategies and tactics. Like a "ninja warrior" fighting with another "ninja warrior," each of them probably knows as much about strategy and tactics as the other. The warrior who has more knowledge and preparation about the opponent or more advantages over the opponent will win the fight. For instance, U.S. firms have some natural advantages. These are proximity to markets, a common language, cultural ties with consumers and distributors, political leverage, labor's cooperation (especially when their employment is at stake), legal expertise, and public sympathy (when circumstances are explained). These advantages should be fully exploited in retaliating to foreign competitors until they wear out and move out of the market.

For example, to deter the Japanese competition in the U.S. market, IBM used a sting operation where some Japanese computer firms' executives were caught red-handed trying to bribe IBM engineers to obtain

IBM's new product design secrets. Capitalizing on the incident, IBM sued the Japanese firms for industrial spying with an intent to illegally find product information. With a loss of face, the Japanese firms agreed to an out-of-court settlement; the terms included a provision that they (Matsushita and Fujitsu) would not enter the U.S. market for fifteen years with the same product and would pay millions of dollars a year to IBM.

BUSINESS LEADERSHIP

Although some prefer that the government take the leadership role in rebuilding America's competitiveness, economies where businesses assume leadership are usually most successful. In Japan, the multinational firms, not the Japanese government, lead Japanese business expansion. Of course, Japanese businesses invariably have substantial guidance and support from their government.

Harvard's Bruce Scott strongly urges business leaders to take the initiative in the revitalization of the nation's industrial and economic growth: "For U.S. economic strategy to become more competitive in circumstances just short of a crisis, business must take the lead" (1989, pp. 115–121). Scott further points out that in the early 1980s, dozens of U.S. firms were making 85 percent of the world's memory chips and semiconductor executives believed there was no way for Japan, or anyone else, to challenge their lead. By 1988, only a handful of U.S. memory-chip firms was left. U.S. global market shares had shrunk to 15 percent. Japan's share meanwhile had soared past 75 percent.

TOTAL QUALITY MARKETING

Total Quality Marketing (TQMkt) is a quality-integrated application of marketing-mix strategies. It is an enhanced version of the "Four Ps" model in marketing. Market Perceived Quality is a primary measure to evaluate the success of Total Quality Marketing.

What is Market Perceived Quality (MPQ)? Product quality is often mistaken for manufacturing quality where attaining zero defects in manufacturing is important. On the other hand, it is equally important that consumers perceive that a product has a higher quality than its rivals. Also, having an inconsistent quality is as bad as having poor quality. Thus, though some American firms have made substantial quality improvements to their products—Ford in the Taurus, and Chrysler in its minivan, for example—most Americans still perceive that American-made products are inferior to Japanese, German, or other foreign-made products. American consumers usually clamor for the foreign makes. They generally perceive that imports have higher quality than locally made products though this may not always be true. Many

American-made products continue to have worldwide reputations for high quality.

It must be noted that improving product quality is a necessary condition, but not a sufficient one, for effective marketing. One cannot sell a steak without the sizzle or vice versa. Keeping this in mind, Xerox Corporation began an intensive quality-improvement effort in the early 1980s that earned the company the prestigious Malcolm Baldrige National Quality Award in 1989. Quality must add value to sales rather than emphasizing cost reduction (Kano 1993). The quality of marketing is equally important. What if the quality of the marketing is not high though the product itself is of high quality? Any number of marketing mistakes can happen. The price could be too high, distribution could be ineffective, or promotion could be weak. In these instances, customers may choose a lesser-quality product simply because it is better marketed. Therefore, firms must go beyond production and improve the quality of their marketing strategies.

A Total Quality Marketing approach must be taken in which the quality of promotion, pricing, product, and distribution strategies are streamlined, carefully planned, and executed with precision. For example, careless advertising, pricing strategies that do not take competitive reaction into account, or the appointment of distributors without prior evaluation should be avoided at any cost.

CONCLUSION

The threat of foreign competition will not fade away. To neutralize the threat, it is important that American firms work with the government and labor unions, though it is not always possible. American firms must not lose the vigor to compete. The inclination "to compete" must pervade throughout the firm—a commitment toward Total Quality Marketing must prevail from top management down to supervisory levels. Regaining market shares should be the key agenda. This could be difficult once consumers develop loyalty to foreign products. Like Black and Decker and Harley-Davidson, firms must also develop and carry out effective preventive strategies such as Total Quality Marketing to stop aggressive foreign firms in their tracks.

CHAPTER 2

Who Is Stealing Market Shares and What Can Be Done about It?

This chapter evaluates import trade from selected countries such as Japan, Germany, the Southeast Asian NICs, and China to identify who is stealing market shares from U.S. firms.

The purpose of the import analysis is to show trends in imports from countries that are actively exporting manufactured goods to the United States. Obviously, a rich country like the United States needs a variety of goods to sustain its standards of living, but excesses can create problems that complicate our economic well-being. The rub is in the excessive imports of manufactured goods from other countries. Therefore, trade deficits must be closely monitored and controlled.

The primary source of data for the analysis is *U.S. Foreign Trade Highlights Report 1992*, a Department of Commerce publication. Figures are rounded to the nearest whole numbers. The Department of Commerce uses two methods in evaluating imports: (1) Customs value and (2) C.I.F. value (cost, insurance, and freight). The former method is based on value decided by Customs at the port of entry. On the other hand, exporters prepare and report the C.I.F. values. Generally, Customs values tend to be uniform worldwide. Therefore, Customs values are used as the bases for the analyses. Second, imports from certain countries are omitted from the analyses since they do not represent a trade threat at this time. Although Canada is the second largest trading partner after Japan, for example, it is excluded from the analysis. The analysis focuses on the manufactured goods; services, oil, and agricultural imports are excluded.

As Americans keep buying a record amount of foreign goods, the U.S. merchandise trade deficit also keeps widening dramatically. Hundreds of billions of dollars of trade deficit each year reflect across-the-board increases in categories ranging from autos to clothing to VCRs.

Composition and Direction of Merchandise Trade

Of total imports of $533 billion in 1992 (Figure 2.1), manufactured goods comprise 33 percent, machinery 28 percent, transport equipment 16 percent, other imports (oil, etc.) 14 percent, chemicals 5 percent, and agricultural products 4 percent. Manufactured goods of all kinds consist of 77 percent of the total imports.

Conversely they also form 72 percent of the total exports of $448 billion in 1992. Apparently, we import more than we export. This is the rub. Regarding the direction of imports in 1992 (Figure 2.2), Canada contributes 19 percent; Japan, 18 percent; twelve countries of the European Community (EC12), 18 percent; Latin America, 12 percent; East Asian NICs, 12 percent; and other countries, 22 percent. Imports from Japan exceed exports by 7 percent. In $533 billion worth of imports, even a small percentage makes a noticeable difference.

U.S. Exports in 1992 were distributed as follows: the EC12, 23 percent; Canada, 20 percent; Latin America, 16 percent; Japan, 11 percent; East Asian NICs, 11 percent; and other countries, 19 percent.

Figure 2.1
U.S. Imports, 1992, by Product

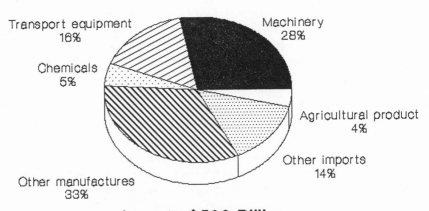

Source: *U.S. Foreign Trade Highlights 1992.*

Figure 2.2
U.S. Imports, 1992, by Country

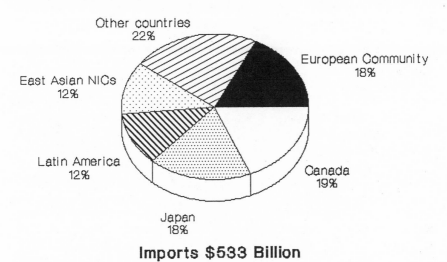

Imports $533 Billion

Source: *U.S. Foreign Trade Highlights 1992.*

TRADE DEFICIT

The U.S. foreign trade deficit has been consistently on the rise, increasing along with the total trade volume. Rough estimates place the cumulative deficit at more than $1 trillion. Such large and chronic trade deficits further debilitate the country's economic, manufacturing, and competitive base. The following analysis evaluates imports by the types and size of merchandise and by the countries for the period studied.

Deficits in U.S. merchandise and manufactured goods began in the early 1970s and gathered momentum into the latter part of the 1980s. Deficits in total merchandise and manufactured goods trade both peaked in 1987 at $152.1 billion for the former and $124.6 billion for the latter respectively (Table 2.1).

Since 1988, for many reasons, there has been a downward trend in trade deficits (Figure 2.3). First, the United States has been pressuring its trading partners to reduce their trade surpluses. Second, because of recession in the United States, there has been a declining trend in imports. Third, responding to U.S. pressures, many Japanese, European, and other foreign manufacturers have set up manufacturing facilities in the United States. For example, Honda, Toyota, Nissan, Mazda, and other foreign manufacturers have set up their manufacturing and marketing activities in the United States. Finally, several American com-

Table 2.1
U.S. Merchandise Trade, 1970–1992 (Billions)

	Total Merchandise			Manufactured Goods		
	Exports	Imports	Balance	Exports	Imports	Balance
1970	43.8	40.4	3.4	31.7	27.3	4.4
1971	44.7	46.2	-1.5	32.9	32.1	0.8
1972	50.5	56.4	-5.9	36.5	39.7	-3.2
1973	72.5	70.5	2.0	48.5	47.1	1.3
1974	100.0	102.6	-2.5	68.5	57.8	10.7
1975	109.3	98.5	10.8	76.9	54.0	22.9
1976	117.0	123.5	-6.5	83.1	67.6	15.5
1977	123.2	151.0	-27.8	88.9	80.5	8.4
1978	145.9	174.6	-28.8	103.6	104.3	-0.7
1979	186.5	209.5	-22.9	132.7	117.1	15.6
1980	225.7	245.3	-19.5	160.7	133.0	27.7
1981	238.7	261.0	-22.3	171.7	149.8	22.0
1982	216.4	244.0	-27.5	155.2	151.7	3.6
1983	205.6	258.0	-52.4	148.5	171.2	-22.7
1984	224.0	330.7	-106.7	164.1	230.9	-66.8
1985	218.8	336.5	-117.7	168.0	257.5	-89.5
1986	227.2	365.4	-138.3	179.8	296.7	-116.8
1987	254.1	406.2	-152.1	199.9	324.4	-124.6
1988	322.4	441.0	-118.5	255.6	361.4	-105.7
1989	363.8	473.2	-109.4	287.0	379.4	-92.4
1990	393.6	495.3	-101.7	315.4	388.8	-73.5
1991	421.6	487.9	-66.3	345.4	388.8	-73.5
1992	448.2	532.7	-84.5	-368.5	434.3	-65.9

Source: Adapted from *U.S. Foreign Trade Highlights 1992*, p. 9.

panies have launched quality management programs that help reduce their import dependence.

As the economic slowdown reached its lowest point in 1991 at $66.3 billion, the trade deficit rose again in 1992, climbing to $84.5 billion for that year. The 1980–1992 data show that as exports rise imports also rise. Therefore, the important thing is how to reduce the trade deficit when it keeps growing continuously. The estimate for the deficit in

Figure 2.3
U.S. World Trade, 1980–1992

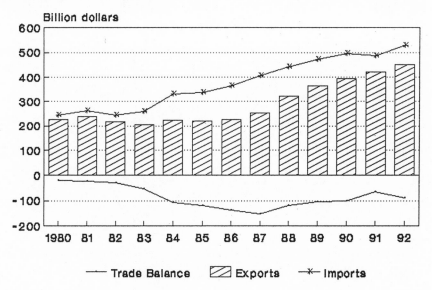

Source: *U.S. Foreign Trade Highlights 1992.*

1993 is on the high side again. To maintain trade balance, steps must be taken to limit the growth of the trade deficit so that it will not go back up again.

Trade Deficit with Selected Countries

A look at the trade deficit with selected countries for 1987–1992 (Table 2.2) shows that Japan leads all other nations, with a six-year average annual deficit of $62.66 billion. We also find that the deficit with China has been increasing since 1987, when it was $2.61 billion to $18.10 billion in 1992. Taiwan's deficit reached its peak in 1988 at $18.87 billion. Obviously, China must be picking up the slack from Taiwan and Hong Kong.

The deficit with Germany has been going up and down since 1988, partly because of the enormous expense of integrating the former East Germany. The trade deficit with Italy is also on the decline, reflecting internal political squabbles in Italy during the past few years. Malaysia is rapidly accumulating a trade surplus with the United States because the United States, Japan, and other countries have greatly increased their business investments in Malaysia in recent periods. Though it

Table 2.2
U.S. Trade Deficit in Manufactured Goods with Selected Countries, 1987–1992
(Billions)

	1987	1988	1989	1990	1991	1992
Japan	-67.60	-67.20	-65.94	-50.10	-59.62	-65.50
China	-2.61	-3.06	-6.02	-10.25	-12.71	-18.10
Taiwan	-15.72	-18.87	-15.66	-13.72	-12.61	-12.02
Germany	-16.64	-13.72	-9.31	-10.78	-6.05	-8.74
South Korea	-11.67	-12.55	-10.65	-8.93	-5.62	-6.09
Italy	-6.03	-5.53	-5.60	-5.53	-4.08	-4.13
Malaysia	-0.66	-1.12	-1.36	-1.34	-1.94	-3.60
Thailand	-0.21	-0.68	-1.32	-1.49	-1.31	-2.41
Hong Kong	-6.55	-5.36	-4.52	-3.84	-2.41	-2.07
Singapore	-2.14	-2.33	-1.72	-1.99	-1.48	-2.02

Source: Adapted from *U.S. Foreign Trade Highlights 1992*, p. 44.

declined in 1989 and 1991, the deficit with Singapore was on the rise again in 1992. Thus, the U.S. trade deficit is generally on the rise with these countries. Whether the deficit is due to U.S. multinationals which operate from other countries is a different question. Also, one cannot attribute all the deficits to U.S. multinationals. Multinational corporations from Japan and other countries also operate in Malaysia, Thailand, Hong Kong, Singapore, and China.

Total Imports from World and Individual Countries

Imports from world and individual countries have been consistently on the rise for the last two decades. The data from 1986 through 1992 (Table 2.3) show that 1992 imports reached $532.7 billion. This is a 9 percent rise from 1991. Significant rises are seen from DCs, Japan, EC12 countries, LDCs, East Asian NICs, and China. Fifty-nine percent of the imports come from DCs, showing that most trade happens between developed nations. Although LDCs represent 36 percent of imports, much of it is oil and raw materials.

Leading Imports from DCs

Motor vehicles, special vehicles, and motor vehicle parts comprise $65.24 billion of the total imports from the DCs (Table 2.4). Other lead-

Table 2.3
U.S. Total Imports from Individual Countries, 1986–1992 (Billions)

	1986	1987	1988	1989	1990	1991	1992
World	365.4	406.2	441.0	473.2	495.3	487.9	532.7
DCs	246.0	256.6	277.7	290.0	297.4	292.3	313.4
West Europe	89.9	95.6	100.6	101.9	109.0	102.6	84.7
EC12	75.8	81.3	85.0	85.3	91.9	102.3	110.8
France	10.1	10.7	12.5	13.0	13.2	13.4	14.8
Germany	25.2	27.2	26.5	25.0	28.2	26.2	28.8
Italy	10.6	11.0	11.6	11.9	12.8	11.8	12.3
U.K.	15.4	17.3	18.0	18.3	20.2	18.4	20.1
LDCs	117.2	141.1	152.7	169.2	180.4	175.0	192.0
E.Asian NICs	46.1	57.7	63.0	62.3	60.1	59.3	62.4
South Korea	12.7	17.0	20.1	19.7	18.5	17.0	16.7
Singapore	4.7	6.2	8.0	9.0	9.8	10.0	11.3
Taiwan	19.8	24.7	24.7	24.3	22.7	23.0	23.0
China	4.8	6.3	8.5	12.0	15.2	19.0	25.7

Source: Adapted from *U.S. Foreign Trade Highlights 1992,* pp. 15–18.

Table 2.4
Leading Manufactured Goods Imports from DCs, 1988–1992 (Billions)

	1988	1989	1990	1991	1992
Motor Vehicles	43.40	41.63	42.55	42.00	42.78
Motor Vehicle Parts	13.93	14.50	13.74	12.27	13.32
ADP Machines	9.02	7.13	7.68	9.20	11.52
Special Vehicles	7.73	8.39	8.10	7.97	9.14
Telecommunication	5.44	6.87	6.69	7.25	7.12
Paper Products	7.15	7.44	7.51	7.09	6.91
Aircraft	4.88	5.30	5.70	6.94	6.94
Thermionic Valves	5.15	6.25	5.82	6.61	7.91
Engine Parts	2.57	3.78	4.79	5.05	5.82
Electrical Machinery	3.83	3.74	3.79	3.59	4.09

Source: Adapted from *U.S. Foreign Trade Highlights 1992,* p. 75.

ing imports consist of automated data processing (ADP) machines, thermionic valves, telecommunication gear, aircraft, paper products, engine parts, and electrical machinery.

Leading Imports from Japan

Machinery and transportation equipment form the bulk of the imports from Japan (Table 2.5). The United States imported about $75 billion worth of these in 1992. The five-year average is $72 billion. Motor vehicles alone average about $20 billion for the last five years. ADP machines and their parts, telecommunications equipment, cathodes, and sound recorders are other top imports.

Leading Imports from the European Community

Machinery and transportation equipment are the principal imports from the European Community (Table 2.6), averaging $38 billion for the

Table 2.5
Leading Manufactured Goods Imports from Japan, 1988–1992 (Billions)

	1988	1989	1990	1991	1992
Chemicals	2.40	2.37	2.39	2.71	3.17
Manufactured	7.34	7.35	6.84	6.63	6.44
Machinery and Transportation	70.02	73.40	69.17	71.10	74.72
Miscellaneous Manufactured	8.40	8.75	9.33	9.21	9.78
Motor Vehicles	20.20	20.26	19.55	20.67	20.11
Automated Data Processing (ADP) Machines	6.74	5.52	5.92	6.84	8.59
Telecommunication	3.94	5.33	4.97	5.27	5.00
Cathodes	3.51	4.37	3.76	4.17	5.01
Sound Recorders	1.35	3.32	3.14	2.84	2.94
ADP Parts	1.89	3.89	3.45	3.52	3.76

Source: Adapted from *U.S. Foreign Trade Highlights 1992*, p. 79.

Table 2.6
Leading Manufactured Goods Imports from the European Community, 1988–1992 (Billions)

	1988	1989	1990	1991	1992
Machinery and Transportation Equipment	36.68	36.20	39.29	37.32	40.98
Miscellaneous	12.68	13.24	14.16	13.07	13.74
Chemicals	9.09	9.19	9.74	10.42	12.07
Commodities	3.24	3.60	4.62	4.32	4.87
Motor Vehicles	8.07	6.74	7.54	5.81	6.62
Aircraft	3.10	3.45	3.22	4.05	4.53
Engines	1.80	2.93	3.65	3.95	4.75
Special	2.44	2.77	3.67	3.40	3.87
Motor Vehicle Parts	2.58	2.47	2.48	2.11	2.10
Measuring Instruments	1.36	1.10	1.11	1.50	1.90

Source: Adapted from *U.S. Foreign Trade Highlights 1992*, p. 89.

last five years. Miscellaneous manufactured goods, motor vehicles, engines, aircraft, motor vehicle parts, and measuring instruments are some leading imports from the EC countries.

Leading Imports from Germany

Major imports from Germany consist of machinery and transportation equipment, followed by manufactured goods, piston engines, special vehicles, motor vehicle parts, electronic diagnostic apparatus, and printing machinery (Table 2.7).

Leading Imports from LDCs

Machinery and transportation equipment lead in the imports from LDCs (Table 2.8). Other top imports are manufactured goods, footwear, textiles, women's wear, ADP machines, telecommunication, and radio receivers.

Leading Imports from East Asian NICs

Hong Kong, Singapore, South Korea, and Taiwan are the principal East Asian NICs. Machinery and transportation equipment, miscella-

Table 2.7
Leading Manufactured Goods Imports from Germany, 1988–1992 (Billions)

	1988	1989	1990	1991	1992
Machinery and Transportation Equipment	16.72	15.00	17.09	15.46	17.19
Manufactured Goods	3.29	3.13	3.26	2.96	3.00
Chemicals	2.70	2.86	3.12	3.30	3.71
Miscellaneous	2.40	2.41	2.73	2.67	2.84
Motor Vehicles	6.50	5.05	5.87	4.02	5.90
Piston Engines	0.80	0.61	0.95	0.89	0.90
Special Vehicles	0.50	0.54	0.89	0.76	0.84
Motor Vehicle Parts	1.01	0.92	0.77	0.59	0.63
Electronic Diagnostic Apparatus	0.37	0.49	0.51	0.54	0.59
Printing Machinery	0.44	0.49	0.48	0.49	0.48

Source: Adapted from *U.S. Foreign Trade Highlights 1992*, p. 99.

Table 2.8
Leading Manufactured Goods Imports from LDCs, 1988–1992 (Billions)

	1988	1989	1990	1991	1992
Food and Animal Products	11.44	11.76	12.45	12.35	12.33
Chemicals	2.83	3.05	3.43	3.71	4.14
Manufactured Goods	18.17	17.90	17.03	16.50	17.84
Machinery and Transportation Equipment	46.02	48.62	49.76	52.22	61.23
ADP Machines	6.41	6.93	7.70	8.73	10.78
Footwear	6.45	6.10	6.32	5.52	5.26
Textile	3.89	5.10	5.11	5.41	6.37
Women's Wear	4.60	5.07	5.31	5.34	6.18
Telecommunication	4.23	4.39	4.48	4.47	5.09
Radio Receivers	2.80	2.53	2.19	2.39	2.69

Source: Adapted from *U.S. Foreign Trade Highlights 1992*, p. 125.

neous manufactured goods, ADP machines, thermionic valves, ADP parts, toys, and apparel are some leading imports from these nations (Table 2.9).

As a newcomer to the export marketing game, China is doing extremely well. Imports from China increased fourfold within the last five years. Miscellaneous manufactured goods, machinery and transportation equipment, toys, footwear, manufactured goods, women's wear, textiles, vanity wear, and men's clothing are some leading imports (Table 2.10).

As stated earlier, there is no doubt that the United States needs a variety of goods from the rest of the world to maintain its quality of life and its high standards of living, but it must not overdo importing manufactured goods to the extent of bankrupting itself with huge trade deficits that it may be unable to reduce. Also, it must be noted that by carelessly shifting industries to other nations the United States is not only losing employment, income, and multiplier effect but also creating problems of social unrest and economic instability that are associated with jobs and incomes of the people. When people do not have jobs, they do not have incomes; therefore they resort to all kinds of activities to get by. The crime rate goes up, and social unrest reaches its peak. Things can simply "go bad" for the country, merely because we are not watching the broad trends in trade, industry shifts, and so forth. According to the

Table 2.9
Leading Manufactured Goods Imports from East Asian NICs, 1988–1992 (Billions)

	1988	1989	1990	1991	1992
Chemicals	0.72	0.74	1.02	1.12	1.28
Manufactured Goods	6.72	6.06	5.95	5.85	6.08
Machinery and Transportation Equipment	27.44	27.74	26.52	26.74	29.73
Miscellaneous	26.27	26.11	24.76	23.40	23.06
ADP Machines	5.47	5.86	6.64	7.45	8.61
Thermionic Valves	3.29	3.84	3.94	4.00	4.66
Footwear	4.89	4.31	4.21	3.26	2.49
Apparel	2.57	3.32	2.83	2.84	1.09
ADP parts	1.11	2.17	2.45	2.53	3.40
Toys	3.13	2.96	2.47	2.37	2.40

Source: Adapted from *U.S. Foreign Trade Highlights 1992*, p. 159.

Table 2.10
Leading Manufactured Goods Imports from China, 1988–1992 (Billions)

	1988	1989	1990	1991	1992
Chemicals	0.23	0.27	0.34	0.39	0.51
Manufactured Goods	1.14	1.33	1.48	1.73	2.29
Machinery and Transportation Equipment	1.15	1.98	2.42	3.26	4.48
Miscellaneous Manufactured Articles	4.73	7.01	9.39	12.13	16.67
Toys	1.07	1.76	2.22	2.73	3.86
Footwear	0.34	0.72	1.48	2.53	3.40
Women's Wear	0.60	0.88	1.20	1.33	1.73
Textiles	0.60	1.03	1.06	1.13	1.46
Vanity Wear	0.43	0.56	0.70	0.90	1.10
Men's Coats, Jackets, etc.	0.34	0.48	0.67	0.72	0.99

Source: Adapted from *U.S. Foreign Trade Highlights 1992,* p. 203.

Department of Commerce estimate, on average, 19,100 jobs result for every $1 billion of merchandise exported. More than 70 percent of American industry now faces foreign competition within the U.S. market (Cateora 1993, p. 35).

CORE ISSUES

A major issue is that Japan's large trade surpluses with the United States are causing trade friction between the two countries. In response to pressure from Washington, Japan has been decreasing its surplus with the United States in the past few years. This has been of no use because America's trade deficit with Japan in recent years is increasing again. This is because of the following reasons: Japan is not only shifting its manufacturing to the United States but also is routing its exports through Thailand, Malaysia, or other countries where it has established manufacturing facilities. By classifying manufactured products as parts and accessories, Japan and other leading surplus countries disguise the nature of their manufactured goods exports. This enables them to appear as inconspicuous as possible.

Another major issue is that China is entering international trade. In less than a decade, China's trade grew rapidly—from around $1 billion in 1985 to $18 billion in 1992. This is attributable to China's aggressive export marketing strategies coupled with its continued status as a most favored nation. Despite China's questionable human rights policies and use of prison labor in manufacturing exported goods, President Clinton extended the status for one more year in 1993; and it will be annually considered after that.

Taiwan's leading role in foreign trade is admirable. A country with 40 million people has multiplied its per capita income ten times in less than a decade—from $500 to $5,000. Taiwan's exports are primarily apparel, toys, computers, telecommunication equipment, and electronics. Taiwan takes advantage of the Chinese immigrants in the United States as a marketing arm to expand its trade with the United States. Low labor costs and aggressive marketing overseas are Taiwan's major strengths.

Over $30 billion of America's trade deficit in 1987 resulted from imports of traditional products—steel, cars, machinery, television sets, and clothing from European countries like West Germany, France, Sweden, and the Netherlands. Most workers in these countries are paid higher wages, have more social benefits, take longer vacations, and work fewer hours than American workers. With the proper investment strategies, the United States could have positive trade balances in these products with these countries (Magaziner 1989, p. 101).

The nations of South Korea, Taiwan, Hong Kong, and Singapore were responsible for over $30 billion of America's trade deficit in 1987. Over 75 percent of U.S. imports from these nations come from U.S.-owned or subcontracted plants, and are sold under American labels. Although wages and benefits average only $2 to $3 per hour in these countries, many products imported from them could be made competitively in the United States (Magaziner 1989, p. 19).

Germany's trade with the United States has generally been in double digits until 1991 when it dropped to $6.05 billion as a result of the enormous expenses Germany had to incur in uniting with the former East Germany. It is expected that the unified Germany will play a greater role in international trade in the future. Germany's manufacturing strengths lie in original and innovative design and high-quality goods.

South Korea, unlike Taiwan, has invested substantially in heavy industries like shipbuilding, steel manufacturing, and automobiles. Its exports peaked in 1988 when the United States accumulated $12.55 billion in deficits. Since then, the deficit has been slowing because of U.S. pressure to reduce it and the U.S. recession. South Korea is not as sound as Taiwan because large borrowing to invest in heavy industry had to be repaid, partly through export earnings.

The declining trend in Italy's trade deficit with the United States reflects the general recession in both countries. Italy mirrors Germany and other Western European nations in that respect. Though imports from Hong Kong have slowed, China has taken up the slack. Thailand's deficit has increased. Malaysia and Singapore also show substantial increases in the deficits because of their more aggressive pursuit of foreign investment and their export marketing efforts.

The Free Trade Dilemma

America is in a dilemma regarding to what extent it should follow free trade tenets that it so strongly advocated in the past. America has been leading the pack on free trade for quite some time. Consequently, many Americans believe in free trade, and our trade policy is based on the laissez faire doctrine. However, the free trade doctrine is not adopted by our trading partners with equal vehemence. They raise more tariff and nontariff barriers against imports coming into their countries while they enjoy free markets in the United States. They profit by exploiting the vast open markets of the United States. Arguments for and against free trade are growing every day as the U.S. economy staggers. Ross Perot, who will probably be an independent presidential candidate in 1996, is clearly against the North American Free Trade Agreement under which the United States, Canada, and Mexico will have a common market with tariff and nontariff restrictions removed. Perot and other protectionists believe that the United States has more to lose from NAFTA than to gain. Several hundreds of thousands of jobs will be immediately lost to Mexico as industries rush to establish more factories there. The manufacturing labor cost in Mexico is about $2.00 per hour, and there are none of the costly programs such as industrial safety, health care, and pensions prevalent in the United States.

Similar sentiment is expressed by Ravi Batra in his book *The Myth of Free Trade: A Plan for America's Economic Revival* (1993). His arguments can be summarized as follows:

1. America became a free trade nation in 1973 for the first time in its three-century-long history.
2. Ever since then real wages have been declining. By 1992, they had fallen by almost 20 percent, and if increased taxes are considered, the real wage had reduced by a third.
3. Throughout U.S. history, even during the Great Depression, the real earnings rose with rising productivity. From 1973, however, though productivity has continued to rise, wages have tumbled. This is the carnage of free trade.
4. Today free trade costs America $300 billion in lost wages and over five million in lost manufacturing jobs.
5. Rising productivity and falling earnings typically plague agriculture. Since the free-trade year of 1973, however, the horrors of farming have become the

horror of American industry. This phenomenon may be called the "agrification of America" in that the entire U.S. industry has been afflicted with the blight of agriculture in the past two decades.

6. Historically America's industrial might was built not by free trade but what may be called "competitive protectionism," which blends high tariffs with intense domestic, but not foreign competition. This is also the secret formula behind the startling success of Japan, Korea and the newly industrialized countries of Asia. In the past, affluent countries used protectionism to build their industrial base. If the United States had listened to free traders, America would not have become the industrial giant that it was until the 1970s.

7. Many economists today blame the Hawley-Smoot Tariff Act of 1930 for deepening the Great Depression, a conclusion that is totally false, because tariffs rose only during 1931 and 1932, and then steadily fell, while the Depression lasted that whole decade. High tariffs generated the "roaring twenties."

8. Free trade helps only when it stimulates manufacturing; when it hurts manufacturing, the country suffers. Because of the eroding industrial base in the United States and thriving industries abroad, every country except America has benefited from the American policy of free trade.

9. International trade creates worse pollution problems around the world. Trade requires long-distance transportation, which in turn guzzles oil or energy, emitting vast amounts of toxins in the process. Free trade maximizes global trade and therefore pollution. To minimize environmental degradations, international trade should be minimized.

Batra's Alternate Economic Plan

Economic policy should maximize domestic competition but not foreign competition, which may be predatory. Similarly, it should minimize trade, but maximize the import of foreign investment and technology so that goods can be produced at home without long-distance transportation. Free investment, not free trade, should thus be our goal.

On February 17, 1993, President Bill Clinton presented his economic plan before a joint session of Congress, calling for sharply higher taxes and modest spending cuts to reduce the budget deficit. In some way, this plan was an echo of Ross Perot's.

While deficit reduction is a laudable goal, the Clinton plan would not create high-paying manufacturing jobs because it retains the policy of free trade. In fact, real wages would continue to fall for the reasons stated earlier. An alternate plan would be as follows:

1. Raise the tariff on imports from 5 percent to 40 percent.

2. Simultaneously increase domestic competition by breaking up the industrial monopolies such as GM, Ford, GE, IBM, and others.

3. Encourage foreign firms to set up new ventures rather than buying the existing concerns.

4. Raise government spending on research and development.

5. Ban mergers among giant firms.

This plan would divert the demand from foreign goods to homemade goods, generating millions of high-paying manufacturing jobs at home and increasing the wages in the process. Simultaneously, enhanced domestic rivalry among American businesses would curb the potentially inflationary effects of tariffs. Foreign companies would establish new ventures in the United States to avoid high import duties. High tariffs would generate good revenue, about $200 billion over four years and thereby sharply reduce the budget deficit.

In the same way, other countries should also encourage competition from within rather than allow foreign competition to enter and destroy domestic firms.

Though there has been a declining trend in import trade since 1989, it is difficult to predict whether this trend will continue in the long run. Japan and the Southeast Asian NICs will continue to be dominant players in the U.S. import trade. To avoid criticism, Japan has been redirecting its exports to the United States through neighboring countries like Thailand or Malaysia, where the Japanese have been setting up factories and getting into joint ventures. China, a new aspirant in the game, is rapidly increasing its exports to the United States. Finally, to reduce trade deficits, the United States must use pressure on countries that have built up sizable surpluses with the United States. The United States should also export more of its products and services to these countries.

Thurow's Perspective

Lester Thurow, dean of the Business School at Massachusetts Institute of Technology, has these comments about the twenty-first century (1993, pp. 28–29). He says the twentieth century is a century of niche competition and the twenty-first century will be a century of head-to-head competition.

The nineteenth century is remembered as the century of Great Britain, which was the dominant economic power. The twentieth century will be remembered as the century of the United States. In terms of the calendar, the twenty-first century has not yet quite begun, but a future economic historian looking back will date the end of the twentieth century early. Just as the fall of the Berlin Wall marked the end of the old contest between capitalism and communism, so the integration of the European Common Market will mark the beginning of a new economic contest in a new century. At that moment, for the first time in more than a century, the United States will become the second largest economy in the world. This reality will signal the start of the competition for domination of the twenty-first century (Thurow 1993, pp. 24–25).

In broad terms, there are now three equal contenders—Japan; the European Community, centered in its most powerful country, Germany; and the United States. Measured in terms of external purchasing power (how much can be bought if one's income is spent abroad), the per capita GNP of Japan and Germany is a little bit larger than that of the United States. In many areas, the United States is no longer a leader.

Today's rules for the international economic game, the GATT (General Agreement on Tariffs and Trade)–Bretton Woods system, were written after World War II and built on the realities that existed a half-century ago. They were designed to help most nations in the industrial world rebuild almost from scratch after World War II. These rules succeeded, but their very success altered the nature of the system. Rules, procedures, and institutions designed for a unipolar world do not work in a multipolar world. As a result, the system that governed the world economy in the second half of the twentieth century will not be the system governing the world economy in the first half of the twenty-first. A new system of quasi trading blocks employing managed trade will emerge.

In the future, sustainable advantage will depend more on new-process technologies and less on new-product technologies. Industries of the future, such as biotechnology, will depend upon brainpower. Man-made comparative advantage replaces the comparative advantage of Mother Nature—natural-resources endowments—or history—capital endowments (Thurow 1993, pp. 15–16).

The next half-century will be a competitive-cooperative three-way economic game between Japan, Europe, and the United States. In jockeying for the competitive advantage, they will force each other to adjust. To mutually prosper, they must cooperate to create a world economy that works and a global environment that allows them to survive and to enjoy what they produce (Thurow 1993, p. 17).

Although there has been a mixed record of economic development since World War II, the successes have vastly outnumbered the failures. With foreign aid and an easily accessed American market, most Third World countries grew from 1950 to 1960 as they had never grown before in all of human history. Except perhaps a dozen countries, mostly in Africa, the per capita standards of living everywhere else are much higher than they were in 1950.

While the ultimate post–World War II goal was that countries become just as wealthy as the United States, probably no one believed that this was really possible. Naive or not, what was then put in place—the GATT–Bretton Woods trading system, the Marshall Plan, the European Coal and Steel Community—worked better than anyone then could have expected. Forty-five years later there are several countries just as wealthy as America. Some Third World countries are on the verge of making it into the First World. Europe is integrating. The communist-dominated economies are now moving toward capitalism and adopting the democratic systems used in Western Europe.

Building upon the economic muscle of Germany, Western Europe is patiently developing into an economic giant. If this bioengineering can continue with the eventual addition of Middle and Eastern Europe, all Europe could eventually become an economy more than twice as large as Japan and the United States combined. In the Pacific, a Japanese economic tiger arose from the ashes of World War II. Emulation led to the birth of four little capitalistic dragons (Korea, Taiwan, Hong Kong, and Singapore) on the Pacific Rim.

From everyone's perspective, replacing a military confrontation with an economic contest is a step forward. No one gets killed; vast resources do not have to be devoted to negative-sum activities. The winner builds the world's best products and enjoys the world's highest standard of living. The loser gets to buy some of these best products—but not as many as the winner. Compared with the military confrontations of the past century, both the winners and the losers are winners in the economic game ahead. Being aggressively invaded by well-made Japanese or German products cannot be compared with being subjected to a military invasion. Nor does it hark back to the German and Japanese military invasions of World War II.

Quite the contrary, the competition revolves around the following questions: Who can make the best products? Who can expand their standard of living most rapidly? Who has the best-educated and best-skilled work force in the world? Who is the leader in investment—plant and equipment, research and development (R&D) infrastructure? Who organizes best? Whose institutions—government, education, business—are world leaders in efficiency?

Military competitions are ultimately wasteful. Resources must be devoted to activities that at best (unused) do not contribute to future human welfare and at worst (used) destroy human welfare. Economic competitions are exactly the opposite. Governments are forced to focus on how they can most efficiently make life better for their citizens. "Economic warfare" is not at all equivalent to "military warfare," despite the use of the word *warfare* in both terms. If the world can reduce its spending on armaments, there is a peace dividend to be had in both the developed and the underdeveloped worlds.

From an American perspective, it is also important to remember that being one of the most wealthy countries in a wealthy world is far better than being the only wealthy country in a poor world—even if Americans are sometimes envious of those newly wealthy neighbors and even if those newly wealthy neighbors sometimes force Americans to rethink how they live.

In the economic contest that lies ahead, the world is not divided into friend or opponent. The game is simultaneously competitive and cooperative. Countries can remain friends and allies yet still want to win.

In the past, American firms dwarfed their competitors; now they find themselves increasingly on the short side. In 1970, 64 of the world's 100 largest industrial corporations were found in the United States, 26 were found in Europe, and only 8 in Japan. By 1988, only 42 were located in the United States, 33 were located in Europe, and 15 were located in Japan. In the chemical industry, the three biggest firms are all found in Germany. Each is at least one-third bigger than DuPont—America's largest chemical company. Except for manufacturing, the same trends exist. Similarly, in 1970, 19 of the world's 50 largest banks were North American, 16 were European, and 11 were Japanese. By 1988, only 5 were North American, 17 were European, and 24 were Japanese. In 1990 there were no American banks in the top 20. In the service sector, 9 of the 10 largest firms are now Japanese.

Starting from approximately the same level of economic development, each country or region now wants the same industries to insure that its citizens have the highest standards of living in the twenty-first century. If it were possible to ask Japan, Germany, and the United States to name those industries they think necessary to give their citizens a world-class standard of living, they would return remarkably similar lists—microelectronics, biotechnology, the materials-science industries, telecommunications, civilian aviation, robotics and machine tools, and computers and software. What was an era of niche competition in the last part of the twentieth century will become an era of head-to-head competition in the first half of the twenty-first. Niche competition is mutually beneficial. Everyone has a place where each can excel; no one is going to be driven out of business. Head-to-head competition is win–lose. Not everyone will get those seven key industries. Some will win; some will lose.

Similar views exist in Germany. On German television in February 1990, Chancellor Helmut Kohl of West Germany issued his counterdeclaration of economic war. "The 1990s will be the decade of the Europeans and not that of the Japanese" (Thurow 1993, p. 31). Implicitly, Chancellor Kohl sees America already out of the game. The same point has been bluntly put by the prime minister of France, Edith Cresson: "There is a world economic war on" (Thurow 1993, p. 31). The rotating head of the EC and foreign minister of Italy, Gianni De Michelis, thinks that Europe is recovering its role as the core of the world economy while others languish in their own problems. The economic competition between communism and capitalism is over, but another competition, between two different forms of capitalism, is already under way. Using a distinction first made by George C. Lodge, a Harvard Business School professor, the individualistic British-American form of capitalism is going to face off against the communitarian German and Japanese variants of capitalism. The Japanese variant of capitalism is examined in detail later, but the essential difference between the two forms of capitalism is their stress on different values as the route to economic success (Thurow 1993, p. 32).

In communitarian capitalism, individuals and firms also develop strategies, but they are built on quite different foundations. The individual does not participate as an individual but must succeed as part of a company team. The key decision in an individual's personal strategy is to join the right team and work with the team as a good team member. In the British-American world, company loyalty is questionable. The individual succeeds as an individual—not as a member of a team. Therefore, job switching is less common in Japan and other countries where communitarianism prevails. In the United States, job switching, voluntary or involuntary, is almost a synonym for efficiency. Turnover rates are viewed positively in the United States and Great Britain.

Here is an example of how Germany controls its economy. When Arabs threatened to buy a controlling interest in Mercedes-Benz a few years ago, Deutsche Bank intervened on behalf of the German economy to buy up the shares that were for sale. This type of intervention protects the managers of Mercedes-Benz from the raids of financial kings. It frees managers from the tyranny of the stock market, with its emphasis on quarterly profits. Bank ownership helps firms plan corporate strategies and raise the money to carry them out. The bank may also fire the managers of Mercedes-Benz if the car maker slips in the auto market, and managers are discouraged from engaging in self-serving activities such as poison pills or golden parachutes that do not enhance the company's long-term prospects.

Both Europe and Japan believe that government should play a role in economic growth. Airbus Industries, a civilian aircraft manufacturer jointly owned by the British, French, German, and Spanish governments is an expression of a pan-European strategy. It was designed to break the American monopoly and get Europe back into civilian aircraft manufacturing. Today Airbus is a big success. It has captured 20 percent of the aircraft market and plans to double production to capture one-third of the world market by the mid-1990s.

There are now several similar pan-European strategic efforts under way, designed to help European firms compete in some major industry. European governments spend from 1.75 percent (Great Britain) to 5.5 percent (Italy) of their GNP in aiding industries. If the United States were to spend what Germany spends (2.5 percent of GNP), it would be spending more than $140 billion to help its industries in 1991. Government-owned firms produced at least half the Gross Domestic Product (GDP) of Spain, whose economy grew the fastest in Europe in the 1980s. In France and Italy, the state sector accounts for one-third of GNP (Thurow 1993, p. 36).

SEEKING NEW SOURCES OF STRATEGIC ADVANTAGE

Historically, individuals, firms, and countries became rich if they possessed more natural resources, were born rich and enjoyed the advantage of having more capital (plant and equipment) per person, employed superior technologies, or had more skills than their competitors. Putting some combination of these four factors with reasonable management was the route to success.

The combination of new technologies and new institutions is rapidly changing these historic views. Natural resources essentially drop out of the competitive equation. Being born rich becomes much less an advantage than it used to be. Technology gets turned upside down. New product technologies become secondary; new process technologies become primary. In the twenty-first century, the education and skills of the work force will be the dominant competitive weapon.

In the twenty-first century, a lack of natural resources could be an advantage. The Japanese have the world's best steel industry, though they have neither iron ore nor coal. To some extent, they are the best precisely because they do not have iron ore or coal. They are not locked into poor-quality, high-cost local sources of supply. There is no need to buy low-quality British coal or American iron ore. They can buy wherever quality and prices are best. Thus, for all practical purposes, natural resources have dropped out of the competitive equation. Having them is not the way to become rich. Not having them is not a barrier to becoming rich. Japan does not have them and is rich; Argentina has them and is not rich (Thurow 1993, p. 45).

While Americans focused on product technologies, Japan and West Germany focused on process technologies. They did so not because they were smarter than Americans but because the United States had such a technical lead in the 1950s and 1960s that it was virtually impossible for either Japan or West Germany to become leaders in the development of new products. They could only hope to compete in existing markets that Americans were abandoning. As a result, Japan and West Germany invested less of their GNP in R&D, and what they did invest was invested more heavily in process R&D. They had no choice (Thurow 1993, p. 46).

What was a good American strategy thirty years ago, a focus on new product technologies, is today a poor strategy. Levels of technical sophistication in Germany, Japan, and the United States are now very different, and reverse engineering has become a highly developed art form. This can be seen in the economic history of three important products introduced into the mass consumer market in the past two decades— the video camera and recorder, the fax, and the compact disc (CD) player. Americans invented the video camera and recorder and the fax; Europeans (the Dutch) invented the CD player; but measured in terms of sales, employment, and profits, all three have become Japanese products (Thurow 1993, p. 47).

American firms have been slow to adopt revolutionary new process technologies such as flexible manufacturing stations, just-in-time inventories, or statistical quality control. The Japanese, on average, are faster at adopting new technologies (Thurow 1993, p. 48).

By using automatic teller machines (ATMs) to deal with the customers, banks are probably more automated than any other industry. Electronic fund transfer systems will eliminate the need for traditional checks. Automated computer systems now trade over half the shares traded on the New York Stock Exchange. Artificial intelligence is being embedded in trading systems even better than those now in use. Financial firms become high-tech manufacturing firms processing money and pieces of paper.

In retailing, those who survive will have the inventory control systems that best reduces costs. Wal-Mart is a good example of a mass merchandiser that installed automated inventory control systems and practiced just-in-time retailing way ahead of its competitors. Retail stores will be directly linked to suppliers to minimize the time lags between a customer's purchase of a particular item and the restocking of that item. Wal-Mart established direct computer links with its major suppliers like P&G, Kellogg, and others. Just-in-time inventories and just-in-time production are the name of the game. The goal will be a seamless web where merchandise is built only shortly before it is delivered and sold (Thurow 1993, p. 49).

Even now, American retailing firms such as The Limited, a clothing retailer, are converting retailing into high-tech competition. The Limited was the first to use high-definition TV across international boundaries so that it would not have to waste time sending buyers to Hong Kong. If The Limited's inventory-control, telecommunication, and CAD-CAM (computer-aided design/computer-aided manufacturing) systems allow it to know what women are buying and put precisely those clothes back on the rack within twenty-eight days while their competitors take six months, they win, and their slower competitors lose (Thurow 1993, p. 52).

Firms must be able to use new computer-based CAD-CAM technologies, employ statistical quality control, manage just-in-time inventories, and operate flexible manufacturing systems. Information technologies must be integrated into the entire production process—from initial designs through marketing to final sales and supporting services such as maintenance. To do this requires the office, the factory, the retail store, and the repair service to have workers with levels of education and skill they have never needed in the past. Every production worker must be taught some principles of operations research to employ statistical quality control. To learn what must be learned, every worker must have a level of basic mathematics. Without statistical quality control, today's high-density semiconductor chips cannot be built. They can be invented, but they cannot be built (Thurow 1993, p. 52).

In the first three decades after World War II, everyone played a mutually beneficial economic game. Imports that looked small to the United States (3 percent to 5 percent of GNP) provided large markets to the rest of the world because of America's great wealth and giant size. Export opportunities were abundant for anyone who wanted to sell in the U.S. market, and the jobs associated with these exports were high-wage jobs by the standards of the exporting countries. Viewed from the American perspective, these imports were not threatening. Foreign market shares were small, and import penetration came in labor-intensive, low-wage industries that were being phased out anyway.

These imports were just an expression of what became known as the "product life cycle." America would invent a new high-tech product and learn to mass produce it. Gradually, the product would shift to being a mid-tech product, best produced in mid-wage countries such as Japan or Europe, from where it would eventually move as a low-tech product to low-wage countries in the Third World.

The United States did these functions not because it was altruistic, although it might have been, but because, as the world's largest economy, it had more to gain from an open global economy than anyone else. The United States believed it could not be prosperous unless the world was prosperous and everyone had equal access to raw materials and markets.

Balancing U.S. trading accounts was not a problem. The United States could grow farm products that other countries badly needed, supply raw materials, such as oil, that the rest of the world did not have, and manufacture unique high-tech products, such as the Boeing 707, that other countries could not build. America's exports did not compete with products from the rest of the world. They filled gaps that others could not fill. In the jargon of today's strategic planners, each country had a noncompetitive niche where it could be a winner. America grew rapidly; the rest of the world grew even more rapidly.

The unique high-tech products the rest of the world could not build have disappeared in a world of technical parity. They can be manufactured in many other places. What in the past was a temporary cyclical trade deficit became a permanent structural trade deficit.

In response, slowly, trade is increasingly being managed by governments. Nontariff import barriers are rising everywhere. In the United States the percentage of American imports subject to nontariff restrictions has doubled to 25 percent in the past decade. At the leading edge of technology, the semiconductor pact effectively turns semiconductor chips into a managed sector; and at the lagging edge of technology, the ever-expanding multifiber agreement keeps textiles in the managed sector. Autos, an intermediate technology, have been in the managed sector for more than a decade. The door to the market of first resort is slowly closing.

The trends are clear. America has made special agreements with Canada and Mexico. Europe talks about associate memberships in the European Community for the remaining nonmember countries in Western Europe and some of Middle Europe. Migration pressures from North Africa are also leading Europe to a Mexican-style agreement with the countries of North Africa by which it will become Europe's preferential low-wage manufacturing area. Bilateral negotiations, prohibited under GATT and leading to principles very different from those of most favored nation, are under way everywhere (Thurow 1993, p. 59).

The American market cannot forever absorb the exports from the Third World. At some point, the United States should generate a trade surplus to pay interest on its accumulated international debts. When it does so, it will cut back on its foreign purchases and go through a period where its market is effectively closed to developing countries (Thurow 1993, p. 62).

Leaving travel and license fees aside, America's 1990 service export to foreigners amounted to only $27 billion. Financial services were seen as a boom area, but U.S. exports never exceeded $5 billion. The semiconductor agreement between the United States and Japan guarantees the United States more than 20 percent of the Japanese market, but no provision is made for the Europeans. Outsiders do not get equal access, and the special privileges given to one are not given to all.

Every country is now unilaterally judging its own trade disputes—no country more so than the United States. One of the GATT–Bretton Woods institutions, the International Trade Organization, was never created. The need to judge trade disputes and enforce decisions resolving those disputes has become more obvious in recent years. Increasingly, countries are making themselves judges of their own trade disputes. When this happens, multilateralism ceases to have any real meaning.

In the empire-building firm, profits are the means to the end of a larger empire—a constraint. The goal is market share. A profit-maximizing firm will devote its higher profits to individual consumption; an empire-building firm will devote its higher profits to investment in expanding its empire.

CONCLUSION

Trade analysis clearly shows the nature and extent of the problems American firms must resolve in the future. In the twenty-first century, both the game and the rules have changed. Therefore, the United States cannot rely on old-fashioned strategies. New strategies must be created to establish U.S. leadership, to regain the market shares lost to foreign competitors, and to fill the coffers of American firms with profits.

CHAPTER 3

SWOT Analysis:
A Simple but Effective Tool

This chapter describes a SWOT (Strengths and Weaknesses, and Opportunities and Threats) analysis of U.S. and foreign firms. SWOT analysis is a basic analytical tool in management that has become popular in recent years.

SWOT analysis is often used by strategic planners and top management in developing competitive strategies. It is typically used to decide corporate strategies and to make product or market level analyses. Here we extend its application to compare and contrast strengths and weaknesses of U.S. business firms with those of competing foreign business firms.

Though the analyses seem to identify only broad trends, SWOT analysis as a technique has the capacity to analyze information in depth depending on the objectives of the users. Thus, by a comparison of strengths and weaknesses and opportunities and threats with those of the competitors (as shown in Figure 3.1), effective strategies and tactics can be developed to combat foreign competition. This versatile technique can also be used in analyzing any two firms or two groups of firms from different countries. Strengths and weaknesses are internal factors of a firm, in contrast with the opportunities and threats, which are external factors (Kotler 1988, p. 50).

1. U.S. firms represent those currently affected (including firms that face the threat in the future) by foreign competitors (automobile and computer firms, for example).

2. Foreign firms represent Japan, East Asian NICs (Korea, Taiwan, Hong Kong, and Singapore), and Western European firms that strongly compete for share and profits in U.S. markets.

To keep the focus of the analyses limited to important issues, only critical selected factors are discussed and analyzed.

Figure 3.1
SWOT Analysis: United States versus Foreign Firms in U.S. Markets

U.S. FIRMS

Strengths	Weaknesses
1. Better market access	1. Short-term orientation
2. Cultural affinity	2. Negligence of quality
3. Technology	3. High wages and overheads
4. Large assets	4. Lack of government support
5. Best infrastructure	5. Inertia
6. Satisfactory image	6. Multilayered management

Opportunities	Threats
1. Vast domestic market	1. Foreign competitors
2. Growing markets	2. Protected markets
3. Trade with communist bloc	3. Technology pirating
4. Hi-tech markets	4. Foreign trading firms
5. Joint ventures	5. Rising business costs
6. Worldwide financing	6. Laws and regulations

DISCUSSION

A cursory glance at the SWOT analysis of U.S. and foreign firms reveals the following salient features.

Strengths of U.S. Firms

1. *Access to U.S. markets.* American firms have instant and better access to vast U.S. markets.

Figure 3.1 (continued)

FOREIGN FIRMS

	Strengths		Weaknesses
1.	Government support	1.	Distance to markets
2.	Large cash reserves	2.	Cultural differences
3.	Quality image	3.	Lack of local markets
4.	Low-interest finance	4.	Rising costs
5.	Business-labor-government cooperation	5.	Poor Infrastructure
6.	Cheap labor	6.	Lack LDC friends

	Opportunities		Threats
1.	Rich markets	1.	Protectionism
2.	Growing world markets	2.	Nationalism
3.	Overseas investment	3.	U.S. retaliation
4.	Former U.S.S.R.	4.	Home competitors
5.	LDC markets	5.	Rising costs
6.	Hi-tech markets	6.	Labor shortages

2. *Cultural affinity with markets.* The fact that U.S. firms can obtain better terms from distributors and suppliers and can promote their products and services to U.S. consumers better than foreign firms because of common cultural heritage, ties, and language should be used for their greatest advantage.

3. *Modern technology.* Computers, aerospace, fiber optics, telecommunications, chemicals, and other high-technologies are a major asset for U.S. firms. Technology must be safeguarded from pirating by other countries. Newer technologies should be developed through research and acquisitions. In addition, many American firms have stronger research and development capabilities and orientations than their foreign counterparts.

4. *Large assets.* Many firms—including such giants as GM, AT&T or IBM—have substantial physical assets and considerable management experience, as well as marketing knowledge and good will. Dormant assets must be con-

verted to cash to provide capital for modernization and launching marketing warfare.

5. *Best infrastructure.* The United States has the world's best infrastructure—excellent transportation, public and private warehousing, banking, insurance, telecommunications, and advertising facilities. American firms should use these facilities to the maximum in interacting with markets faster and more effectively than the competition.

6. *Satisfactory image.* Despite cries about declining quality, firms like IBM, P&G, and Coca-Cola still maintain good product quality and service. Therefore, many U.S. firms still project a positive image. Exceptions may be found in a few industries like automobiles, textiles, cameras, and electronics (radios, televisions, VCRs) where foreign products are known for better quality. These strengths must be better used by U.S. firms in their fight against foreign competition.

Weaknesses of U.S. Firms

While maximizing these strengths, U.S. firms should find ways to minimize their weaknesses: first, by addressing declining quality more seriously; second, by reducing costs of labor through modernization and worker training; third, by tying management compensation to market share rather than to profits; fourth, by seeking less distrust from labor and government; fifth, by becoming more enthusiastic and aggressive in fighting foreign competition; and finally, by trimming existing multiple layers of management.

Opportunities for U.S. Firms

There is no dearth of opportunities in the decade of the 1990s. There exist a vast domestic market, a growing international market, and markets from the Eastern bloc countries, including the former Soviet Union countries. Markets in computers, chemicals, aerospace, transportation, and energy continue to expand; and these markets must be fully exploited. In the same manner, American firms should not hesitate to develop joint ventures with foreign firms when it is advantageous for them—like GM's pact with Toyota to make Geo cars in California.

American firms should also take advantage of the international financial markets in Tokyo, London, and Paris to secure low-interest loans or equity financing. Firms must develop a global view for their business and operations by participating in joint ventures, direct investment, licensing, and other foreign market entry methods. Last, American firms must innovate products that are suitable to other countries (GM's world car, for example), just as foreign competitors do.

Threats to U.S. Firms

1. *Foreign competitors.* The Japanese and other foreign firms (including the LDCs like India and Brazil, as well as the newly liberated Eastern bloc) will continue to pose a threat to U.S. firms. Without a doubt, foreign competition is increasing and becoming more aggressive.

2. *Fragmented markets.* The continued trend toward market fragmentation requires a rapid transition from traditional manufacturing methods to flexible manufacturing processes. Rising business costs and consumer resistance to further price increases will become a double threat to marginal firms.

3. *Restricted foreign markets.* Many foreign markets, including those of Japan and the European Community (EC), are not fully open to American-made products. Therefore, reciprocity in trade, both in quantity of goods and in dollar volumes, should be achieved with each of the major trading partners.

4. *Technology pirating.* However careful U.S. firms are, technology pirating is still a major threat. Japanese and Asian firms are quick to copy U.S. technology and flood U.S. markets with improved products, with our own technology.

5. *Large Asian trading companies.* Japanese and Korean trading companies (such as Mitsubishi and Samsung), with their vast financial, manufacturing, purchasing, and distribution resources, have developed distinct advantages over American firms. They buy raw materials cheaply because of their worldwide supplier connections, gather market intelligence, and efficiently distribute their products to global markets. American firms are currently faced with far more threats than opportunities compared to foreign firms.

SWOT ANALYSIS OF FOREIGN FIRMS

Strengths

1. *Government support.* Foreign firms receive full support from their governments to achieve their overseas marketing objectives. The Japanese Ministry for International Trade and Industry (MITI) and the Japanese Export Trade Organization (JETRO), for example, help promote industries that are export oriented. The Japanese government systematically discourages declining industries like radio and television while allowing high-tech industries to grow.

   The Korean and Taiwanese governments also back their businesses. These governments help businesses by giving subsidies, helping them in getting long-term, low-interest loans, sharing research and development costs, helping to obtain market research information, and restricting imports and entry of foreign businesses that hurt their industry and economy.

2. *Large cash reserves.* Large cash reserves now held by Japanese, Taiwanese, and Korean firms allow them to spend more on research and development to produce new and improved products. These reserves also enable them to take risks in spending large sums for advertising and promotion. Foreign

firms do not have the high costs of borrowing that American firms have, thus they are able to earn larger profits.

3. *Quality image.* Foreign firms take full advantage of the quality image their products have earned over time because of highly automated modern factories and use of modern production and management methods.

Foreign firms have substantial advantages over American firms, especially in their ability to achieve higher levels of quality and productivity and in the availability of low-cost labor and financing. These foreign firms take full advantage of these benefits in effectively competing with American firms in U.S. markets.

Weaknesses of Foreign Firms

1. *Physical distance from U.S. markets.* An obvious disadvantage for foreign firms is the physical distance to U.S. markets. Transportation costs range between 5 percent and 20 percent of the product's selling price. But through bulk shipments, modernized loading and unloading facilities, containerization, and utilization of U.S. Foreign Trade Zones to save on duties, foreign firms can lower their physical distribution costs and overcome part of this weakness.

2. *Cultural differences.* Another major weakness is their lack of similarity in culture and language. By engaging American distributors to sell their products, employing American engineers to design such products as cars, using American advertising agencies to promote products, and lobbying in Washington and state capitals, foreign firms can overcome these weaknesses. To reduce initial marketing costs, some foreign firms also use expatriates living in the United States to gather market information and to distribute their products until permanent arrangements can be made.

3. *Lack of large domestic markets.* Lack of large domestic markets can become a major weakness, particularly when world marketing opportunities begin to constrict because of recession or protectionism.

4. *Growing shortage of skilled workers.* Because of tremendous industrial expansion, there is a growing shortage of workers in Japan and in Asian NICs. With rapid industrialization, demands for higher wages are increasing as worker expectations rise. When the demands are unmet, strikes occur, disrupting production and increasing costs. Political unrest, which often occurs in South Korea, disrupts production flows.

5. *Limited infrastructure.* As industries keep growing, foreign firms find that they become trapped by a limited infrastructure. Japan, for example, is only as big as California with 140 million people inhabiting the country.

6. *Lack of other friendly countries.* Finally, as a result of their reluctance to help needy developing countries with economic assistance in the same manner as the United States and other Western countries, firms in Asian countries may loose the support and markets of LDCs.

Opportunities for Foreign Firms

1. *The rich U.S. and Western markets.* Continued growth in American and Western markets provide opportunities for foreign firms for a variety of new products. Economic integration of the kind happening in the EC and in the emerging North American trading block provides immense trading and investment opportunities in large, borderless megamarkets.

2. *Overseas investments.* Direct overseas investment is another opportunity. Several states in the United States invite foreign firms to establish direct investments or joint ventures, an opportunity that foreign firms cannot overlook. It was reported that forty-eight states maintain trade and investment promotional offices in Tokyo to cultivate Japanese businesses.

3. *Huge Chinese market.* Because of proximity and cultural affinity, it is easier for Pacific Basin countries to penetrate markets of China.

4. *Product patents.* Because of their patent holdings in high-tech products like VCRs, camcorders, and the like, Japanese firms like Matsushita and Sony will continue to enjoy market opportunities.

Threats to Foreign Firms

A major threat to foreign firms is the rising wave of worldwide protectionism. When their own economic stability is threatened, U.S. and Western nations will try to regulate their free markets. Many U.S. firms like IBM and Harley-Davidson are effectively controlling foreign invasion of their markets. Both Xerox and Black and Decker have vigorously fought foreign firms and regained their lost market shares. In addition, foreign competitors are likely to face increasing competition from firms from their own country.

THE JAPANESE INVESTMENTS IN THE UNITED STATES

Here are some views on the Strengths and Weaknesses of the Japanese Investors:

Strengths

- Abundant capital
- Low cost of funds
- Strong domestic base
- Technological leadership
- Access to Asian markets
- Choice of targets
- Long-term outlook
- Lack of shareholder accountability

Weaknesses

- Unfamiliarity with local markets
- Lack of U.S. management skills
- Language
- Long-term outlook
- Lack of experience with merger and acquisition (M&A) deals
- Unfamiliarity with financial analysis techniques. (Partner 1992, p. 125)

Religion plays a vital role in Japan (Partner 1992, p. 25). Although Japan's state religion was traditionally Shintoism, early rulers did not suppress Buddhism or Confucianism. Maoist Japanese are a Buddhist–Shintoist–Confucian blend in their religious outlook. Modern Japanese put great stock in their complex religiousness. Factories have animistic shrines and protective deities. Shintoism contributes the ideal of loyalty to one's clan, group, or company. In the tradition of the Shintoist Samurai warriors, the Japanese value sacrifice for the sake of their leaders— whether in government or business. They accept apologies and atonement for one's mistakes or breaches of responsibility. Buddhism contributes the idea of mentorship, in the master–disciple model of Zen Buddhism, also the ethics of frugality, silent meditation, and formality. Confucianism instills values of duty and family piety. Collectively, these value systems contribute to Japan's success and make Japan a unique realism and what it is today.

To help understand the business culture of Asian countries, Partner catalogs six commandments of Asian commercial practice:

1. The collective comes first.
2. For every person, a social rank and station.
3. Let there be harmony (at least on the surface).
4. No person shall "lose face."
5. Relationship first, business later.
6. The rules of propriety and ceremony shall prevail. (1992, p. 52)

The best defense for American firms is to become more aggressive and enter foreign competitors' markets even at the risk of initial losses. To contain foreign competition, there is no substitute for understanding other countries' methods of doing business. Equally important is effective control of import and export trade. Finally, as Nimgade's study points out, American managers have some unique qualities: They are open-minded, objective, flexible, hardworking, aggressive, hard-nosed, and practical (1989, pp. 98–105). These virtues must be put to use in combating foreign firms.

American firms should get their act together and put up a common front against competition. It is unfortunate that a joint venture like U.S. Memories, Inc., which was set up by American firms to effectively compete with cooperative Japanese firms, did not succeed. Such cooperative approaches in many future technologies such as high-definition television (HDTV), laser technology, genetics, fiber optics, superconductivity, and the like are becoming imperative for global market success. It is not clear to what extent the U.S. businesses can develop such cooperative and integrative approaches to effectively compete with foreign firms. It is necessary to develop specific strategies to incorporate quality into product, promotion, pricing, and distribution areas. In the next two chapters, such quality-driven marketing mix strategies are discussed in detail.

One reason German companies are freer to invest in long-term plans is the nation's banking system. Banks are more than lenders, they often own equity too, giving them a stake in supervising companies in the long term.

In Japan, large manufacturing companies tend to stay focused on production and marketing even in tough times. During the mid-1980s, Japanese electronic firms chose to keep semiconductor prices low, despite billions of dollars worth of losses, so they could keep building world market share. Their smaller, stock-market dependent U.S. rivals could not afford the stakes, so the Japanese came out the winners, and are now making good profits.

The threat of hostile takeovers is another source of pressure on U.S. managers, forcing them to emphasize high stock prices over high investment. Companies that invest aggressively in five-year growth plans are becoming takeover targets because their profits temporarily go down (Magaziner 1989, p. 305).

JAPAN: THE MAJOR CHALLENGER

Japan has been a major trading partner and the major competitor of the United States for decades. For many years, the United States has sustained a trade deficit with the Japanese. In recent years, however, both the trade and the deficits have grown enormously. The trade deficit with Japan in 1990, at $41.8 billion, was 38.5 percent of the total U.S. deficit. Although in dollar terms it is below the 1987 peak of $56.3 billion, it is hardly surprising that there is considerable opposition in Congress to the Japanese trade surplus with the United States (Partner 1992, pp. 1–2).

Investments in the United States by foreign nations are generally divided into two categories: direct and indirect. Indirect investments include purchase of stocks and bonds, including U.S. Treasury securities. The Japanese have been major investors in these securities in recent years, effectively underwriting the U.S. budget deficit.

Net purchases of U.S. securities by the Japanese totaled $17.4 billion in 1990, but the volume of Japanese investments is much greater still. During the 1980s, the U.S. government has come to rely on Japanese investors to purchase one-third of all newly issued U.S. debt.

Although net indirect assets of the Japanese far exceed their direct investments, the direct investments have caused the most furor. These are often highly visible purchases such as the acquisition of Rockfeller Center in New York City or Columbia Pictures. It is about these investments that critics claim we are "selling out" to Japan or that America is losing her sovereignty.

Japanese direct investments have grown rapidly in the past decade. According to the Commerce Department, in 1980 net investments totaled a mere $4.7 billion, or 5.7 percent of total foreign direct investment. By 1990, that number had grown to $83.5 billion, or 20.8 percent of the total. The compound annual growth rate was 33.3 percent.

Nor, in spite of a slowdown in 1991, does the trend show any sign of declining. The relatively strong yen coupled with massive cash surpluses generated by Japan's export success have put Japanese companies in an overwhelmingly strong financial position (Partner 1992, p. 3).

Japanese investment in the United States went through an unprecedented growth phase during the 1980s. In the process, Japanese money has become a controversial topic, leading to an increasing anti-Japanese sentiment. It seems that the larger the issues get, the more polarized the sides become. On the one hand, an irate American public feels Japan has gone a step too far yet wishes the United States could catch up with Japan's achievements. On the other, the Japanese public feel they have been unfairly singled out and blamed for America's own weaknesses. Some influential Japanese have responded with tough rhetoric aimed at "standing up" to the Americans. An example is the recent hard-hitting best-seller, *The Japan That Can Say No* (Partner 1992, pp. i–x). It must be remembered that we are not at war with Japan. Japan and its Asian trading partners are the fastest growing markets of the 1990s. America needs Japanese money. Dealing with the Japanese does not mean selling out.

Today's gray-suited, travel-stressed American corporate executive might well wonder what became of the country's former dominance. As he or she sits in a featureless hotel room entering penny-pinching calculations into a laptop computer, it is probable that the suite next door is occupied by a group of laughing Germans or Japanese here to outbid the American in tomorrow's negotiations. While the United States is not a poor or a defeated nation, the undisputed leadership it enjoyed in previous decades has passed out of its hands. Of the nations that have risen to claim their "place in the sun," Japan is foremost on people's tongues (Partner 1992, p. 16).

Japanese Investment in the United States

These are some arguments for and against Japanese investment in the United States. Although, Japan is not a major investor like Canada, the United Kingdom, Holland, or others, caustic remarks against Japanese investment seem to pervade.

Arguments against:
1. Japanese trade practices are unfair.
2. Japanese industries are out to destroy their American rivals.
3. Japan is stealing key technologies and reducing America's defensive capabilities.
4. Japanese employers are racist and sexist.
5. The Japanese incursions into the United States are part of a plot to gain world domination.

Arguments for:
1. Japanese companies are creating jobs in the United States.
2. Japanese companies are improving the quality of manufactured goods.
3. Our politicians and businesspeople are begging the Japanese to invest.
4. The Japanese pay top dollar.
5. National boundaries are irrelevant in a global economy.
6. Americans are racially motivated when they condemn the Japanese.
7. The Japanese are good citizens.
8. Japanese investment cannot harm the U.S. economy.

Some see a double standard in the attitudes of politicians and the American public. The American politicians go to Japan asking the Japanese to invest in the United States and then turn around to criticize the Japanese investment. Somehow they do not seem to exhibit a similar behavior toward West European investment in the United States, although these investments sometimes may not benefit the United States.

The so-called "trophy investments" which have caused so much criticism (e.g., Columbia Pictures or the Rockfeller Center) were not initiated by the Japanese. It is Americans that sold these properties; therefore, they are the ones that should be criticized rather than blaming the Japanese for buying these properties (Partner 1992, p. 112).

Evidently, the furor over high profile Japanese investments in the United States is more emotional than real. In fact, Japanese companies tend to invest in overseas assets with highly specific goals in mind. Japanese buyers generally look for some proprietary asset, such as a niche or brand name, or a well-established dealer network. Investments in brand can be rewarding to both sides, as the Japanese open their domestic distribution channels more widely to manufactured products from other countries.

CONCLUSION

It is easy to blame others for our failures. Perhaps something good has come out of this competition. Without competition, new products and quality products would not have been made available to consumers around the world. The important thing is how America can rebuild its fortune using more modern concepts of Total Quality Marketing.

Clearly, Americans need to exploit their unique strengths—rich domestic and growing world markets, modern technology, and an excellent infrastructure. Also, they should acknowledge the strengths of foreign firms such as government support and cooperative and cheap labor and learn to deal with foreign firms. Foreign firms have distinctive weaknesses in tapping American markets. They have to transport goods from great distances and transcend cultural barriers and prejudice. However, some foreign firms have established manufacturing in the United States to overcome this disadvantage. Most of all, foreign firms cannot win the loyalty of the American consumers. They will patronize products that are made in the United States when American firms make efforts to observe the principles of Total Quality Marketing, discussed in the later chapters.

CHAPTER 4

The Market Share Mystique

This chapter contains a discussion of the theoretical background of the market share strategy. What is market share? Why is it important? How is it measured? What are key considerations in using the market share strategy?

Generally, a firm that increases its market share in an industry can earn more profits than a firm that has a low market share (Buzzell and Wiersema 1981). This observation applies to both domestic and global markets. A metaanalysis of 276 market share–profitability findings from 48 studies shows that on average, market share greatly affects business profitability (Szymanski, Bhardwaj, and Varadarajan 1993). Therefore, it is important for firms to have a better understanding of the subject of market share.

The positive relationship between market share and profits is also evident in the PIMS (Profit Impact of Marketing Strategies) study of the Marketing Science Institute. Furthermore, the tremendous success of Japanese firms using market share as their primary strategy proves the point. Japanese firms have employed the market share strategy quite successfully. Initially they adopt a low-price, high-quality product-marketing strategy. After getting a certain portion of the market share in an industry, these firms often switch to a high-price, high-quality strategy and thus enhance their profits.

Market Share in Globalized Markets

Typically, market share notions both in theory and practice are viewed in connection with a domestic market. In today's globalized markets, however, such domestic market–oriented thinking is becoming obsolete for strategy development and application. In the past, when the U.S. market was the largest, overseas markets were considered unimportant.

Today, more major players in many product markets think and act in terms of global market shares instead of purely domestic market shares. Such global orientation in management thinking has significant implications for competitive strategy with a focus on market share. Companies with high market shares in a domestic market may sometimes mistakenly feel that their market shares are less vulnerable to foreign competitors' attacks—especially if such foreign competitors initially have a low domestic market share.

But if those foreign competitors have reasonable market shares on a global scale, they can prove to be formidable competitors. This is exactly what is happening with many foreign competitors in the U.S. market, whether they are from Western Europe, Japan, or the NICs. Foreign competitors from these countries, through their global market shares, are likely to enjoy economies of scale, experience curve effects, and reap the benefits of other phenomena. In other words, competitive strengths of foreign firms should not be judged on the basis of their low market shares in the U.S. domestic market but should be evaluated on the basis of their total global market shares and associated strengths.

Similarly in evaluating their own competitive strengths, U.S. companies should consider their global market shares along with their domestic ones. Global market shares and ability to compete successfully in diverse market environments are true indicators of competitive prowess in today's globalized markets. In this context, Prahalad and Hamel (1990, pp. 79–91) enumerate the following situations where multinational corporations (MNCs) must maintain some level of market share to manage their business successfully.

1. A minimum market share for worldwide cost competitiveness. This refers to calculating, capturing, and holding a minimum market share in both the domestic market and world markets to become cost effective in production.

2. A minimum market share for national profitability. This refers to obtaining the minimum market share necessary for profitable operations within a single country.

3. A minimum market share necessary for effective retaliation. This refers to a minimum market share necessary to influence cash flow of foreign competition on its home turf. Thus, for example, by achieving only 2 or 3 percent penetration in the competitor's market, the firm may not adversely influence a large foreign MNC with a substantial market share.

4. A minimum market share necessary in its home market to reduce risk of attack by foreign firms. As they can offset losses in one market with profits from another, the foreign MNCs (Japanese MNCs, for example) can attack the domestic market share of a U.S. firm with relative impunity. Therefore, the U.S. firm must maintain minimum market share in the U.S. market to minimize risks from foreign competition attacks.

Market share strategy is a long-term objective because it takes a great deal of time to build a sizable market share. American managers tend to follow short-term profit strategies instead of long-term and thus neglect the market share strategy. The concern for short-term profits in American industry is based on stockholders', management's, and Wall Street's obsession with quick return on investment. Furthermore, compensation and reward structures for managers and top management are traditionally based on short-term results instead of long-term achievements.

In building market share, foreign firms, especially Japanese firms, pursue unique ways. They forgo short-term profits, postpone payment of dividends, and reinvest revenues into research and development to create and produce newer, better-quality products that the competition cannot match.

MARKET SHARE THEORY

The basic theory of market share is as follows: Market share of a company in a product market will be proportional to share of "attraction" from its marketing effort to total "attraction" resulting from marketing efforts of all firms in the industry operating in that product market (Bell, Keeney, and Little 1975, pp. 136–141). Thus, a firm's market share expressed as a percentage is share of the market for that firm from total shares of all firms involved in a given product-market category for a given period. For example, market share of foreign automobiles in the U.S. market today is 30 to 35 percent of the total U.S. automobile market.

MARKET SHARE EQUATION

The foreign automobile market share in the United States equals foreign automobile attraction divided by foreign plus U.S. automobile attraction. Mathematically,

$$s_i = a_i / \Sigma a_i$$

where

s_i = expected market share of firm i
a_i = "attraction" resulting from marketing effort of firm i
Σa_i = "attraction" resulting from marketing efforts of the total industry.

According to this equation, once a firm finds its total served market size, it can capture some percentage of the served market based on the distinctive characteristics of its product and marketing abilities. For example, before entering the U.S. automobile market, the Korean Hyundai car manufacturer calculates the minimum market share it can expect and must obtain before such entry. The firm had already captured a 10 percent share in the neighboring Canadian automobile market. With this background, Hyundai's initial expectations were to obtain a market share of 2 to 5 percent in the U.S. automobile market. By launching the Excel model successfully in the U.S. market, the Korean manufacturer could achieve its initial market share goals. To further increase its market share, Hyundai subsequently introduced more expensive models like the Sonata, a larger car with better features than the Excel model.

To predict a firm's expected market share on the basis of the market share equation alone can be difficult because it requires full knowledge of competitors' present and future marketing strategies. Such information is usually difficult to obtain because few competitors publicly reveal any of their marketing strategies.

BENEFITS

This section deals with the benefits, criticisms, limitations, and caveats of the market share strategy. Two important benefits of market share strategy are (1) lower production costs and (2) increased profits.

Lower Production Costs

Large market share holders can reduce total production costs beyond the large scale and experience curve economies. Each time production is doubled, the total cost per unit will fall by a certain percentage (Tull and Kahle 1990, p. 33).

Increased Profits

Results of the PIMS confirm that a positive relationship exists between market share and profits (i.e., increased share leads to increased profits). Profits measured by pretax return on investment (ROI) rise curvilinearly with relative market. The average ROI for businesses with less than 10 percent market share is about 9 percent. On the average, a difference of 10 percentage points in market share results in a difference of 5 points in pretax ROI. Furthermore, businesses with market shares above 40 percent earned an average ROI of 30 percent—three times that of those with shares under 10 percent (Kotler 1988, p. 327).

Firms operating in large markets like those for automobiles or computers need to work harder to retain or increase their market shares. Often, as ROIs are usually predetermined, a 1 percent share gain in a $60-billion automobile market translates to a $600-million sales increase that in turn can lead to increase in profit of $120 million (based on 20 percent ROI rate).

LIMITATIONS

Market share strategy also has some limitations. The cost of increasing the market share can often exceed its real value. There are several factors that firms should keep in mind before pursuing a market share strategy. First, firms should guard against provoking other firms to invoke antitrust action—especially if they are trying to merge with or buy up other firms in the same industry (horizontal integration). Second, a firm with a large market share may have saturated the market, and any further share increases could cost more than benefits received. Third, competitors can get more desperate and fight hard when some firms try to increase their already large market shares. Furthermore, the cost of legal advice, public relations, and lobbying rises with the market share. Fourth, economies of scale will disappear, market segments will become unattractive, buyers will want other sources of supply, and exit barriers become high. Thus, a firm with substantial market share should increase prices to achieve higher profits rather than pushing for further market share. Fifth, market share cannot be further increased because customers may not like the firm; they may be brand-loyal to competitors' products; they may have unique needs that the firm cannot satisfy; or they may prefer to buy less known or generic brands.

KEY CONSIDERATIONS

The following list is adapted from Tull and Kahle's criteria for market share strategy:

1. The company should be in an industry where increased market share can lead to higher long-term profits. Typically, automobiles, computers, and color televisions fall into this category. These are industries where foreign competition is also quite intense.

2. Product(s) should be in an early stage of product life cycle. The underlying objective is to capture substantial market share in introductory stage and harvest profits during maturity stage. The Japanese firm, Matsushita Electronics, has dominant market share for the video cassette recorder market because of its earlier decision to let others like RCA use its VHS patent to produce and market their own brands. Sony's Betamax market is negligible since it did not use a similar strategy.

3. The market should be large and sufficiently price-elastic to allow sizable economies of scale in manufacturing or marketing to result in substantial potential profits.

4. Product(s) should be of good quality compared with those of competitors.

5. After considering relative qualities of products, the company should have either an actual or a potential cost advantage compared to competitors' costs.

6. The company must be willing to devote substantial resources to both product and manufacturing R&D and to plant and equipment improvement and expansion. Japanese firms are adept at this. With increased profits, Japanese firms reinvest in R&D to improve product design and achieve manufacturing efficiencies. Japanese car manufacturers churn out new models with highly appealing designs at competitively low prices. Consider the redesigned 1990 models of Honda Accord or the new Mazda Miata.

7. The company must have, or be willing to get, a marketing capability that is at least equal to that of its nearest competitor.

8. Japanese and Korean manufacturers of electronics have followed a market share strategy superior to that of American firms—low price, high quality, intensive distribution, and frequent high-quality advertisements in the national media.

9. The company needs to be well financed, either from internal funds or from low-interest bank financing that Japanese and Asian manufacturers can obtain from their government-backed banks.

10. Management must be willing to undergo two types of risks: risk of loss of money should market share strategy fail and risk of possible antitrust suits by competitors if the strategy is successful. (1990, pp. 29–35)

Not all these conditions can be met, but the potential effects of the absence of one or more of these ten factors should be considered in planning a market share strategy.

FIGURING OUT MARKET SHARE

A variety of statistical tools and computer models are available to accurately decide market share of existing products. However, estimating market share for new products is difficult since they have no past sales history.

To predict the market share for a new product, four different methods are used: (1) conducting an intention-to-purchase survey, (2) making an estimate based on a judgment of the company's share in a similar market area, (3) using market testing, and (4) using simulation.

Surveys

Intention-to-purchase surveys are not the best predictors of product demand. When introducing new products, however, it is imperative that a firm test the "concept" with a sample of potential buyers. Consumers are given information about the product and its benefits and are then asked about their intention to buy. This method reveals prima facie if there are any major defects in the product idea itself. If so, the firm can modify the product accordingly.

Analogy

Before introducing a new product, a firm reviews the market and estimates percentage market share it can expect by using a similar market situation elsewhere. For example, if market conditions in Mexico and Brazil are similar, the firm can use its knowledge in one market to make predictions of demand for its product in the other country. Though simple to use, the major weakness of this method is qualitative differences between two markets that are usually not considered because of difficulties in estimating them. This can often lead to misleading results.

Market Testing

Market testing has become an important method since it is generally more accurate than the other methods discussed here. Market testing is an expensive and time-consuming process. It costs anywhere from $100,000 to several million dollars, and it takes from six months to several years to conduct. Proctor and Gamble took nearly fifteen years and spent several million dollars before it successfully introduced Pampers. In testing, the firm can use two different stores—one as a standard and another as the controlled environment. By manipulating marketing mix in the controlled store, the firm can develop ideas about the likely market penetration of the product. A major problem with market testing is that competitors can influence test market results by introducing their products in the same test markets to distort results.

Simulation

In simulation, advertisements for the new product are shown to consumers asking them to purchase and use the product, and evaluate its attributes. The rates of trial, repeat purchases, and usage rate, coupled with assumptions about distribution and advertising, are then used to estimate market share. Many consulting firms and advertising agencies use simulated testing. Some firms even have their own test systems. The most important advantage of simulation is that it permits prediction of different market share scenarios under different assumptions.

Most firms use a combination of these methods instead of relying on one. Whatever their individual advantages and disadvantages, the value of experienced managerial judgment cannot be completely overridden.

SPECIFIC MARKET SHARE STRATEGIES

Pitts and Snow (1986, pp. 24–34) discuss four basic strategies to pursue market share: pioneering a business, rationalizing a business, segmenting a market, and revolutionizing an industry. These share-building strategies pose a threat to firms that already have large shares of the market. The strategic challenge for market leaders is to maintain market share against the efforts of smaller competitors to gain it.

GAINING MARKET SHARE:
AN EXPENSIVE PROPOSITION

To gain market share, a small competitor simply needs to enhance the relative attractiveness of its product or service to prospective customers. Many approaches are available, including price reductions, increased advertising, higher product quality, better service, longer warranties, and so on. All these actions are likely to be expensive, and they tend to depress the business' profitability in the short term. Price reductions may be matched by large market shareholders.

Product development can be costly since it takes years to perfect a product before it is introduced to the marketplace. Companies that try to expand market share by manipulating their own marketing mix find the process leading to what is known as "buying" market share. In the 1970s, General Electric thought of getting into the mainframe computer market by buying market shares. Despite its best efforts, GE held only 4 percent of the market share against IBM's 70 percent share. GE had to increase its market to at least 15 percent to make profit. GE would have had to spend $2.4 billion to gain 11 points of market share at the rate of $220 million per share. Therefore, GE sold its mainframe business to Honeywell.

Product Life Cycle

As this example illustrates, buying market share can be very expensive. A small-share competitor must look carefully for special opportunities to gain share less expensively during the various stages of the product life cycle—introduction, growth, maturity, and decline. Four strategies are possible as shown in Table 4.1.

STRATEGY 1: PIONEERING A BUSINESS

What kind of strategies can a business use in its introductory stage?

Environmental Opportunities

An emerging industry is generally characterized by many small competitors, several of which are pursuing different technologies and product types. Product quality and reliability usually fluctuate both within and across firms, and prices are generally high. Therefore, the customer base typically is small, with only a few innovative customers purchasing these early product offerings.

There are opportunities for market share gain here. First, all the competing firms are small, so no competitor has a significant scale or experience advantage over the others. A small-share firm that moves adeptly can thus gain a size or experience edge relatively quickly and inexpensively. Second, common structural barriers to expansion, such as access to suppliers or distribution channels, are likely to be fewer in a new business than in a mature one. A small-share competitor can thus expand easily. Finally, the competitive dynamics of an emerging industry also present business opportunities. The absence of large, entrenched competitors means that the competitive game probably will not be marked by strong retaliative behavior. All competitors are simply trying to perfect initial product designs, not fight each other by using such strategies as price cutting or advertising blitzes. Only later, as the market grows, are these retaliatory weapons commonly used.

Risks

Pioneering a business entails risks. One risk is market demand. Some markets look promising at first only to disappear later. For example, Westinghouse pioneered mass transit systems during the 1960s in anticipation of growing demand. It lost most of its investment when demand failed to appear. Other firms experienced similar disappointments in synfuel. During petroleum shortages of the early 1970s, synfuel energy was expected to have a brilliant future, and many companies invested heavily to develop alternative energy sources. A general decline in the price of oil, however, undercut the potential market; and most of the pioneering firms were unable to recover their investments.

Pioneering also involves technological risk because several technologies usually vie for supremacy during a product's infancy. One of these technologies probably will prevail and become the industry standard. A pioneer that has championed an outmoded technology is likely to lose its investment. This happened in the early stage of the automobile industry where steam, electric, and internal combustion engine technologies initially competed. Steam technology quickly lost, however, and its pioneers—including the maker of the famed Stanley Steamer—failed. Electric cars and their manufacturers met the same fate.

Technological risks are prevalent today in emerging industries and in mature industries based on high technology. For example, in its first year as a publicly owned company after the British government divested it in 1982, Amersham International was a huge success in the medical instrument business. The small company used its expertise in radioac-

Table 4.1
Strategies for Gaining Market Share

Characteristics	Pioneering Business	Rationalizing a Business
Stage of product life cycle	Infancy	Growth
Basic environment	Small, new market	Rapid market growth
Sources of opportunity to gain market share	Few competitors with scale or experience advantages Little competitive retaliation	Insufficient capacity among competitors to satisfy market demand Early market leaders more concerned with rising sales than with market share Shifting requirements for competitive success Attraction of first-time customers who have not yet established loyalty
Strategic risks	Market demand does not materialize Miscalculation of eventual technology	Investing too little or paying too much to develop market share Threat of new competition from outside the industry
Functional policies Product design and engineering	Multiple, sometimes redundant technologies Continual experimentation with product features and configurations	Adoption of a single technology Adoption of a standard set of product features and configurations Substitution of lower-cost materials and redesign for less expensive manufacture

Segmenting a Market	Revolutionalizing an Industry
Maturity and decline	Maturity and decline
Slow or plateauing market growth	Steady or declining market
Existence of dif- ferences among buyers	Fundamental environ- mental changes
Possible retaliation from market leaders	Rapid adaptation by market leaders
	Entry by outside competitors
Differentiate the business from approaches of market leaders in one or more key respects (technology, product design, cost, variety, quality, service, etc.)	Differentiate the business from approaches of market leaders in one or more key respects (tech- nology, product design, cost, variety, quality, service, etc.)

Table 4.1 (continued)

Characteristics	Pioneering Business	Rationalizing a Business
Process engineering and manufacturing	Building prototypes High Labor content General-purpose equipment Low-volume, short production runs	Increasing workflow efficiency Automation Special-purpose equipment Low-cost mass production
Marketing and distribution	Specialty distribution channels, word-of-mouth or other limited advertising, and premium pricing	Mass distribution channels, mass media advertising, and declining product prices
Organization structure	Multiple self-contained units such as project teams, product groups, and divisions	Single functional structure to achieve efficiences in production and marketing, often supplemented with matrix units or brand managers
Management processes	Flexible planning for rapid reallocation Decentralized decision making and control	Emphasis on long-range product planning More centralized decision making and control

Source: Pitts, Robert A., and Charles C. Snow (1986). *Strategies for Competitive Success.* New York: John Wiley & Sons, pp. 32–33. Used with permission from John Wiley & Sons.

tivity to make medical diagnostic kits based on radioactive materials. In less than a year, the technology changed substantially as many customers switched to kits using nonradioactive products. Amersham's lead was quickly eclipsed by newer competitors employing nonradioactive technology.

Implementing the Strategy

A business that chooses to pursue the pioneer strategy must carefully develop functional policies in three areas: technology, product engineering, and distribution. A soundly conceived policy for technological

Segmenting a Market	Revolutionalizing an Industry
Organization structure, management processes, and people fitted to the chosen differentiation approach	Organization structure, management process, and people fitted to the chosen differentiation approach

research and development is crucial because a business that miscalculates the eventual technological basis of the industry's product or service may not be able to catch its more perceptive competitors. Therefore, pioneers often explore simultaneously all relevant technologies so that they obtain expertise in whatever method ultimately emerges as the industry standard.

RCA used this approach in the video recording equipment business. Rather than concentrate on a single technology, it chose to develop simultaneously both tape and disc videocassette recorders. Obviously, this dual-track effort was costly. However, it significantly reduced the likelihood that RCA would miss an opportunity for market share leadership because of technological misjudgment. As the market developed, disc technology proved to be a failure. However, RCA is a leader in videotape recorders. Had RCA pursued only disc technology, it would have suffered a setback such as that experienced by Amersham International.

Pioneers must also investigate alternative product designs and distribution approaches. Most new products can be designed and distributed in different ways, and the possible combinations of product design, technology, and distribution method may be large. Therefore, a pioneering business must experiment and plan in each of these areas—single and in combination—until the "right" blend emerges. Of course, it is too early in the product life cycle to find out conclusively a successful mix of product engineering, technology, and distribution, so the pioneering competitor must maintain its flexibility by forging ahead with deliberately redundant thrusts.

By pursuing these types of functional policies, pioneers can be "first to the market" with a new product or service. To be first consistently, however, pioneers must develop organization structures and management processes that allow them to prospect systematically for new opportunities. Many companies have wrestled with the organizational and administrative problems associated with moving a new product from conception to commercialization. Their efforts have produced no universally acceptable solutions, but the basic dilemma seems clear: Which group should be responsible for the development of the new product; what resources should be provided to this group; and how should the group interact with the rest of the organization?

Every successful new product must eventually be commercialized, designed, produced, marketed, and distributed to customers regularly. Performing all these activities consistently requires a considerable investment of time, people, money, and other resources. Who should be given total responsibility for these tasks? In answering this question, a company will often look to its existing line organization where there is the most experience in manufacturing, distribution, and so on. However, as many companies have found, this approach can have serious drawbacks. For example, line managers' attitudes about a new product can be a problem. If most of these managers believe that the product has little market potential, then they may not pursue its development aggressively. Or they may take such a short-term view of the product's profitability that they quickly abandon the product after its introduction to the market.

A second problem involves cannibalization. If the new product appears likely to change or perhaps obsolete the current product line, forces in the organization may emerge to slow or even stop the product's development.

A third concern is the size of the organization being considered as a candidate for the product's development. If the organization is already quite large, it is possible that the new product will not achieve the visibility and attention it requires to be successful.

The alternative to assigning the product to an existing organization is to create a separate organizational unit with specific responsibility for the product and to provide the unit with all the required resources. Such units are project teams, product groups, and divisions. These structures provide the needed speed and flexibility for continuous product innovation because each product line or project can be managed autonomously.

Probably more than any other company, Hewlett-Packard has shown the benefits of this structural approach. HP began with the notion that high returns were possible by moving products from basic design to the market quickly. The fundamental organizational unit at HP is the product division, an integrated, self-sustaining organization with a great deal of independence (the company today has over 60,000 employees in more than 60 divisions). To successfully pursue this approach, a company must use people management practices—especially those involving hiring, placement, and rewards—that are appropriately matched with the company's considerable decentralization. Human resources decisions are usually made with emphasis on team "ownership" of products from conception through commercialization and on rewards for successful innovations (not simply position in the hierarchy). As much as possible, mistakes are absorbed rather than punished so that organization members are continually motivated to experiment with new ideas.

Defending against Pioneers

Faced with aggressive share-building efforts by pioneering companies, how should a market leader respond? Most important, early leaders in a new business must recognize that the benefits of its leadership are likely to be limited. Generally, two factors serve to constrain the normal competitive advantages of market leadership. First, as described earlier, no competitor is likely to possess a major scale or experience advantage because of the small size and newness of the market. Second, even the limited advantages enjoyed earlier by early market leaders probably will be temporary because initial strategic choices about technology, product design, distribution channels, and so on, are subject to rapid change. For these reasons, most market leaders are in approximately the same position as their smaller competitors. Therefore, they too must think and act like pioneers, pursuing similar policies and managing similarly.

STRATEGY 2: RATIONALIZING A BUSINESS

According to the logic of the product life cycle, a product moves out of its infancy when demand for the product begins to grow rapidly. The growth stage is reached when the experience gained by pioneering companies enables them to increase quality and reduce price to the point where large numbers of buyers are willing to enter the market.

Environmental Opportunities

A market's rapid growth provides a small competitor four special opportunities for market share gain. First, during this period, dominant competitors may have insufficient capacity to satisfy market demand. A small competitor that intelligently adds to its capacity has a chance to grab a sizable share increase. Second, early market leaders sometimes do not respond aggressively when smaller competitors make gains during the growth period. Their docility may come about because market growth enables leading competitors to increase sales though they are losing share to smaller rivals. Content with rising sales, market leaders allow smaller competitors to pursue their competitive strategies with relative impunity.

A third opportunity involves the shifting requirements for success of a growing business compared to a new one. At this stage of the life cycle, a product must be simplified and produced for everyday use. Videocassette recorders and personal computers are recent examples of products that have gone through this simplification process. Also, the simultaneous exploration of several technologies must give way to reliable low-cost manufacturing using a single technology.

Last, marketing and distribution approaches must generally be modified. For example, in the early days of major home appliances, washers and refrigerators were sold by specialized appliance dealers. Now appliances are sold mainly in department stores that carry a variety of other merchandise. Personal computers, which were initially sold as kits through mail-order catalogs or in computer specialty stores, are now sold mainly in retail department stores. Most recently, consumer financial planning services are moving through a similar marketing and distribution metamorphosis, as large retailers such as Sears increase their importance as a distribution outlet. Small-share competitors that can meet these new requirements can achieve significant market share gains over earlier pioneers wedded to old-fashioned ways.

A fourth opportunity for market share gain stems from the fact that most buyers in a rapidly growing market are first-time purchasers who have not yet established loyalty to a particular brand. A small competitor seeking to gain market share, therefore, does not have the problem of luring customers away from established buying patterns and preferences. Market share gain becomes much more difficult when industry maturity is reached. At that point, a firm can increase its share of the market only by breaking the habits and loyalties of repeat purchasers, a typically difficult and costly undertaking.

Risks

Making a commitment to develop market share during high growth periods entails risks, of course. One risk involves the amount a business invests to increase its market share. Underfunding the rationalizer strategy is simply wasteful. If the business is not prepared to invest whatever it takes to survive the inevitable shakeout among competitors, it probably should invest available funds elsewhere. On the other hand, a business may pay too dearly trying to develop market share. Westinghouse's large investment in the growing market for nuclear electrical generating equipment is a case in point. To achieve an early sales lead, Westinghouse made a risky promise to prospective customers: It guaranteed to supply them with the nuclear fuel to feed the reactors they bought from Westinghouse. These guarantees ran for many years and committed Westinghouse to supply nuclear fuel from outside suppliers to meet its commitments. This arrangement worked fine as long as the price Westinghouse paid for uranium was below the price it guaranteed its customers. During the late 1970s, the price of uranium skyrocketed, reaching levels far above Westinghouse's guaranteed price to customers.

The liability involved was so enormous that it could have led even a big firm like Westinghouse to bankruptcy. Fortunately, Westinghouse was able to negotiate settlements with most of the customers involved. Nonetheless, these settlements resulted in writeoffs totaling several hundred million dollars. As this illustration suggests, expenditures to develop market share must be carefully weighed against expected payoffs.

A second risk in a growing market is the threat of new competition. For example, because of a spate of acquisitions of small, independent semiconductor firms by large, cash-rich corporations (United Technologies, Philips, etc.), Texas Instruments, the early semiconductor market leader, had to contend with a new set of able and well-heeled corporate owners eager to increase their share of the semiconductor market. Where do these new competitors come from? It is obviously difficult to forecast which firms might enter a given business, but they often come from the following groups: (1) firms not in the industry but able to overcome entry barriers relatively inexpensively; (2) firms that could benefit from one or more synergies by being in the industry; (3) customers or suppliers who might integrate backward or forward; and (4) mergers or acquisitions that might occur, among either established competitors or outsiders. These potential entrants are particularly troublesome competitors not only because they are difficult to identify but also because, as with semiconductors, they are frequently large corporations. As such, they may have access to more resources than the small independents.

Implementing the Strategy

Successful rationalizers must be particularly adept at developing a product after it has been pioneered. This usually requires a substantial shift in the functional policies for product design, manufacturing, and marketing-distribution. For example, whereas the pioneer experimented extensively with product features and technologies, the rationalizer must adopt a single technology and a standard set of product features and forms. The key to achieving a successful product and technological focus is to discern from the many experiments that have occurred during the infancy phase those product features that will be most acceptable to the mass market. A well-known example of this rationalization process is the automobile industry in its early days. The pioneering companies experimented with three competing technologies: steam, electricity, and the internal combustion engine. Henry Ford was perceptive enough to select that combination of technological and product features wanted by the growing mass market for automobiles. Ford's famous Model T quickly became the industry standard and remained so for many years.

A successful rationalizer must also shift its manufacturing orientation. During a product's infancy, the pioneering company's manufacturing system is geared toward building prototypes; therefore, production runs are short. To appeal to the mass consumer, however, a rationalizer must increase its manufacturing efficiency through higher volume, improved work-flow, standardized production operations, installation of automated equipment, and so forth. By making these kinds of changes, Henry Ford achieved low-cost mass production before any other automobile manufacturer. Accordingly, during the years 1909 to 1921, Ford continued to reduce the price of his cars.

Last, a rationalizer must recognize that marketing and distribution of the product will also change at this stage of evolution. During the product's infancy, successful pioneers use specialized distribution channels and marketing approaches to reach small market segments composed of knowledgeable customers. During the growth phase, the emphasis must be on mass marketing and distribution to reach large numbers of first-time buyers. Here also, Henry Ford set the industry standard for distributing and marketing automobiles by anticipating customer needs in locating, purchasing, and mainlining a car. Pioneers had offered their cars to buyers through catalog sales, in retail stores, and through dealers. Ford benefited from these experiments and decided to create a nationwide network of franchised dealerships. This approach is still the standard means of distributing and selling new automobiles.

A more recent example of a successful rationalizer is Matsushita Electric company. Matsushita seldom originates a product, but it usually succeeds in manufacturing the product at a lower cost and marketing it expertly to the mass consumer. For example, in the videotape recorder business, Sony not only pioneered the technology but established its brand name Betamax as synonymous with the product. Given Sony's reputation and its initial leadership in this market, its position was formidable. However, using a strategy that has worked for decades, Matsushita looked for a means of skirting a rival's technological or market lead. The company's own market surveys have shown that consumers wanted longer video capacity than that of the Betamax. Today, Matsushita, selling under the Panasonic and other labels, has become the leading manufacturer of videotape recorders.

Matsushita has over twenty production research laboratories equipped with the latest technology. It analyzes competitors' products and consumer markets extensively and then figures out how to make its own version of a product on a reliable, low-cost basis. It also believes in the importance of market share and experience. When higher production volumes generate cost savings, these are passed on to customers via reduced prices, thus establishing barriers to entry for competitors who find the small margins unattractive. Finally, it promotes its brand names (National, Panasonic, Quasar, Technics) heavily, forges close relationships with distributors and dealers, and innovates in point-of-purchase marketing.

Certain organization structures and management processes lend themselves to the rationalizer strategy. Although variations are many, most rationalizers set up special organizational units and processes focused on market and competitor surveillance, process engineering, and so-called brand or project management. A major competitive advantage obtained by a successful rationalizer is the ability to manage large-volume products rapidly through the sequence of design, manufacturing, distribution, and marketing. As such, brand and project managers play a central role in carrying out this strategy.

For example, Texas Instruments (TI) frequently pursues this strategy in its rapidly growing businesses. TI operates in the electronics industry, covering the same product territory as Hewlett-Packard (HP). It too has many operating divisions, though not as many proportionately as HP, and it also views itself as a leader in new product technology. However, TI believes it can compete not only in the early phase of product development when the emphasis is on uniqueness but downstream as well, when the competitive race goes to the most efficient mass producer.

TI prides itself on its ability to shift organization structure and management processes appropriately given the stage of product's development. New products are carried through the design and early marketing phases in division or project structures, just as at HP. However, their development is more tightly planned, and the process of allocating resources to such developments is closely monitored. Moreover, from the beginning of a new product, its potential for being smoothly produced and marketed is constantly evaluated. When a new product is firmly entrenched, its course is well charted (e.g., target markets are identified and specific objectives for the product are set). Prototype structures and processes give way to more formal organizational and managerial systems emphasizing efficient production.

One common outcome of efforts such as these is to become the industry's low-cost producer. As a growth business matures, market leaders can defend their positions by seeking the lowest-cost position compared with competition, coupled with both an acceptable quality level and a pricing policy geared toward maintaining high volume. Low-cost producers thus take advantage of stabilizing technology and product design by shifting their resources into efficient manufacturing, mass marketing, and distribution and especially by paying strict attention to cost control. Companies that have achieved the status of low-cost producer in their respective businesses include Goodyear (tire and rubber), White Consolidated Industries (major home appliances), South-Western (college textbooks), McDonald's (fast foods), Lincoln Electric (arc welding equipment and suppliers), and Texas Instruments.

Defending against Rationalizers

How can a market leader respond to the efforts of competitors attempting to rationalize a business? Two major approaches are frequently used. For example, Hewlett-Packard, as described earlier, may choose to leave a business if the requirements for holding market share involve low-cost production, mass marketing, distribution, and so on. Thus, sometimes, HP deliberately plans its exit from a market before the product matures. As an experienced pioneer, HP is frequently first to the market, and it charges high prices for a new product. As the market for this product expands, the profits obtained from this approach are largely plowed back into new product research and development, and the product life cycle begins anew. Instead of developing the skills required for the mass production and distribution of a mature product, HP simply leaves the arena to others who possess such skills.

Alternatively, as practiced by Texas Instruments and other companies, a market leader may choose to manage a new product through its growth phase to maturity. Here, it will try to defend its market share by becoming both the low-cost producer and an adept mass marketer. Here the market leader must recognize that the requirements for competitive success will probably shift as the product evolves, and the company must act to take advantage of its size and experience. Apple Computer, for example, is using this approach to defend its share of the personal computer market. It has built a state-of-the-art production facility to achieve low-cost manufacturing, and it brought in as president a highly regarded marketing executive from a consumer products company to guide the firm from a pioneering to a more rationalized competitive approach.

STRATEGY 3: SEGMENTING A MARKET

Consider a business that has missed the two opportunities to gain market share discussed so far. Its market has reached maturity, yet it is still a small-share competitor. What can it now do to improve its competitive position?

Environmental Opportunities

Even mature markets can present opportunities to gain market share. The most common source of opportunity is market differentiation: the existence of differences between buyers and consumers. By this point in an industry's evolution, customers have become knowledgeable about the industry's product or service and more demanding in their preferences. If these preferences vary considerably, a small competitor can focus on a segment of customers whose needs are relatively homogeneous and largely unmet. By achieving strength in that market segment, the small competitor effectively becomes the dominant competitor, obtaining some benefits of market share leadership.

In most consumer and industrial markets, customers have a wide enough range of needs to provide at least some segmentation opportunities. Consider overhead garage door openers, for example. Most customers buy this product from a professional craftsperson who installs and maintains the electric opener. Others, however, are willing to install and maintain the equipment themselves. The Stanley Works has built a very successful business by catering to this do-it-yourself market segment. It sells this product through hardware and other retail stores rather than through the professional installers targeted by most firms in the industry. Stanley's business is still quite small compared to that of the market leaders, but it is the leader of the do-it-yourself segment. As a result, it is the industry's most profitable competitor.

Risks

The major risk a segmenter faces is retaliation by larger competitors whose size gives them an advantage a segmenter can't match. Four factors largely decide the vigor of retaliation. One involves the skills needed to operate in a particular market segment. When these skills are similar to those required by the larger market, a leader can easily move into a segment. However, when they are different, the leader may have difficulty in entering. Consider again the market for overhead garage door openers. To operate successfully in the do-it-yourself segment of that market, a competitor must have access to retail distribution channels and skill in consumer advertising. The Stanley Works is successful in this segment in part because of the lack of these factors among the industry leaders.

A decision by market leaders to enter a segment also will be influenced by their fear of cannibalization. When increased sales in a particular segment come at the expense of sales in the larger market, leaders may avoid the segment, fearing that aggressive effort there will only serve to reduce their sales elsewhere. Fear of cannibalization may explain why Coca-Cola waited so long to come out with Diet Coke, its major entrant in the sugar-free segment of the soft drink market, and why Tab was seldom promoted heavily.

A third factor influencing the likelihood of retaliation by industry leaders is the behavior of a segmenter itself. When a segmenter makes little effort to switch customers from the main market over to its segment, industry leaders are often content to leave a segmenter alone. However, they react quite differently when a segmenter tries to lure their customers away. When this happens, leaders may try to "discipline" the segmenter for its behavior. Seven-Up has learned this lesson the hard way. Following its "ungentlemanly" uncola campaign designed to get cola drinkers to switch to sugar-free, caffeine-free Seven-Up, both Coca-Cola and PespiCo introduced new products and dramatically intensified marketing efforts. Thus, Seven-Up seems only to have succeeded in goading the market leaders into heavier competition; its huge advertising outlays have produced little or no improvement in its market share.

A final factor influencing the vigor with which large-share firms are likely to respond to a segmenter is segment growth. A low-growth segment is much less likely to be pursued aggressively by industry leaders than one whose growth exceeds that of the total market.

Implementing the Strategy

To minimize the risk of retaliation, a segmenter must choose a segment requiring skills different from those of the larger competitors. It must then develop policies to enhance these differences. For example, Control Data Corporation, a successful segmenter in mainframe computers, uses its technological skills to manufacture large sophisticated computer systems that it sells mostly to knowledgeable users such as government agencies and large corporations. This approach allows the company to minimize its efforts in sales, service, and software development—all important skills in the general computer market dominated by IBM.

In the housewares industry, Dansk Designs concentrates its efforts on the expensive "top-of-the-table" market segment. Dansk produces a line of custom-designed tabletop items of "museum" quality for distribution through specialty stores, advertises in luxury-oriented publications, and maintains through a network of craftspeople and manufacturers. The company has succeeded by portraying itself as a maker of artistic, as well as functional, housewares.

Air Products, a manufacturer of compressed gases, originally differentiated itself by eliminating one of the functions normally present in the industrial gas business. Instead of transporting heavy gas containers from a large central plant to its customers, as was the tradition, Custom Air Products built small plants near large gas users and simply pumped the gas directly into their plant. This approach essentially eliminated transportation costs.

Wendy's does not try to compete head-on with the fast-food giant McDonald's. Instead, it offers more variety and higher quality in its product line. Of course, Wendy's also charges higher prices and thus appeals mostly to the over-30 market segment.

Finally, some competitors rely on service or convenience as their primary means of differentiation. For example, the Southland Corporation, owner of a large network of 7-11 food stores, offers customers the convenience of location and long hours. Thus, these stores cater to small-purchase customers who are willing to pay higher prices for items obtainable in large supermarkets.

Defending against a Segmenter

In general, the same concerns that the segmenter has about the market leader's possible entry into its market should govern the leader's choice of a competitive response. That is, market leaders are likely to remain passive toward a segmenter if (1) the market segment is not growing rapidly, (2) the skills required to operate in that segment are substantially different, (3) entry may cannibalize the leader's current business, and (4) the segmenter is not trying to lure away the leader's customers. However, if any of these conditions changes, the market leader should reassess its passive stance.

STRATEGY 4: REVOLUTIONIZING AN INDUSTRY

A small-share competitor in a mature industry can sometimes pursue a more ambitious strategy than segmentation to become the industry leader. The net result may be a true industry revolution, and vivid examples of this phenomenon have occurred throughout American business history.

Environmental Opportunities

The key requirement for revolutionizing an industry is fundamental environmental change that can stimulate rapid growth in a particular market segment. Consider for example, the automobile industry in the 1920s. General Motors's bid to oust Ford as industry leader was vitally helped by many environmental changes taking place then. Automobiles were being driven longer distances and at greater speeds, thus raising consumer interest in auto safety and comfort. Yet Ford continued to offer only the Model T, an essentially open (and therefore dangerous) automobile without significant comfort options. Disposable income was also growing during the 1920s, so more consumers had the means to pay for improvements and distinctive features. Ford, however, continued to base its strategy primarily on low price. By developing "families" of cars suited to a wide range of consumer needs at different prices, General Motors quickly gained a dominant share of the total market and achieved the leadership position it holds today.

Timex caused a similar revolution in the watch industry in the 1950s. Emerging from World War II with no market for its bomb fuses and other mechanical devices, it developed the inexpensive, "disposable" mechanical watch. Timex took advantage of the trend toward more upscale lifestyles in the 1950s. As consumers quickly embraced the idea of having several watches (and watchbands) for different occasions, the company came to realize its role as a mass producer and distributor. It rapidly wrested world watch leadership from the Swiss.

Risks

The most serious risk for an industry revolutionizer is that market leaders will adjust to the new realities before the revolutionizer can achieve a commanding position. If leaders react quickly enough, they can usually maintain both their market dominance and the competitive advantages that go with it. Fortunately for small competitors, market leaders often delay before adapting to major environmental change. If they do, revolutionizers have an opportunity to increase their market share.

What accounts for this delay? Several factors may contribute to it. One involves awareness. The management systems of market leaders are essentially designed to monitor environmental factors that have been important in the past. Riveted upon yesterday's environment, market leaders may miss important developments in other areas. For example, most U.S. electrical manufacturers for years have treated the radio as a product in the mature or even declining phase of its life cycle, starving it of investment funds while devoting attention to other products. Japanese electrical manufacturers, on the other hand, did not view the radio in this way. They considered it important to the consumer's entertainment and lifestyle. The phenomenal success of the Sony Walkman, wristwatch radios, radio-in-pocket calculators, and related products is evidence that Japanese companies were more aware of changing consumer tastes than the traditional U.S. leaders of this industry.

Management assumptions may also play a role. The success underlying market share leadership can confirm managerial beliefs about what it takes to succeed in a particular market. Sometimes, no amount of counterevidence can shake the leader's conviction that the old ways are the right ways. Many airlines executives are convinced that today's travelers require free in-flight meals and entertainment, that they are unwilling to handle their own baggage, and so on. The success of People's Express, which charges passengers for services "à la carte," shows the inaccuracy of this assumption.

Finally, the delayed response by market leaders to the threats of an industry revolutionizer is partly one of will. Even when market leaders recognize change and understand the adjustments required, they still may delay out of unwillingness to obsolete existing assets and skills and to begin business newly under a different set of competitive conditions.

Implementing the Strategy

Like the segmenter, a revolutionizer must be willing to behave quite differently from the industry leaders. Indeed, many revolutionizers start out as segmenters, often as outsiders who simply see a different way competing in a mature industry. However, there is a major difference. Unlike the segmenter, whose competitive advantage lies in dominating a relatively small portion of the total industry, the revolutionizer's initial market segment grows very rapidly. Rapid growing in turn attracts other new entrants to the market, inviting retaliation from major competitors. Therefore, the revolutionizer's strategic risks are potentially much greater than the segmenter's.

A revolutionizer must therefore act with dispatch. Although it is true that the revolutionizer may do some initial experimentation with technology, product design, or distribution, it must be prepared to move quickly through the growth phase or the new, high-growth segment by employing the rationalizer and low-cost producer strategies described earlier. Otherwise, it could gain a significant share of the revolutionizer strategy. This is well illustrated by Iowa Beef Processor's moves in the meat market where both the potential and existing competitors formulate their own approaches to the changed conditions in the industry.

The revolution in the meat packing industry over the last decade has completely revamped the means of killing, chilling, and shipping beef in its bid to become the low-cost producer. Unlike former market leaders such as Armour, Wilson, and Cudahy, which shipped live animals to rail centers (such as Chicago) for slaughtering and distribution, Iowa Beef built modern, highly-automated plants in the sprawling feedlots of the High Plains and Southwest. This saved on transportation costs and avoided the loss that occurs when live animals are shipped long distances. Iowa Beef also cleaves and trims carcasses into final cuts that are boxed at the plant, in that way further reducing transport charges by removing excess weight. Finally, the company has fought hard to keep labor costs down. Today it is the biggest and most profitable meatpacker.

As the Iowa Beef case illustrates, the policies and skills pursued by revolutionizers may reflect aspects of all the competitive strategies previously discussed. Revolutionizers bring a new approach to a segment of mature or declining industry, they grow rapidly when that segment expands, and they may ultimately choose to defend their market position by low-cost production. It is a difficult but potentially profitable approach for a small-share competition faced with a stable or declining industry.

Defending against Revolutionizers

Market leaders have three basic options for responding to the competitive efforts of an industry revolutionizer. The most natural response is to promote ones' traditional approach through actions such as increased advertising, lowered prices, discounts to distributors, and a host of other tactics designed to counteract the revolutionizer's attempt to grow.

A second competitive response is to "harvest" the business. If, for whatever reason, a market leader chooses not to counteract the revolutionizer's moves, it can begin to exit from the business in an orderly fashion by cutting back on investments and thereby extracting larger profits until sales begin to decline. Fortunately for some market leaders, the harvesting periods can be sustained for considerable periods of time.

Finally, a market leader can decide to adjust the new realities created by the revolutionizer. However, as noted, market leaders sometimes are slow to do so. Therefore, it seems appropriate to conclude this chapter by recommending two major ways in which leaders can overcome the inertia described above.

One way is to gain access to new ideas and information that are not likely to come from the existing organization. Common vehicles for increasing the number of fresh perspectives available to an organization are hiring outside consultants, selecting members of boards of directors for their special expertise, forming venture capital committees to evaluate and fund innovative ideas from organization members, sending key managers to executive education programs, and hiring managers and employees from competitors experienced in alternative ways of conducting a particular business.

A second set of actions that can be taken to help overcome the rigidities of market leadership involves the creation of "learning laboratories" within the organization. These are areas where organization members can experiment with new approaches without interfering with the operations of the main system. Such potential learning arenas include geographically isolated plants, acquisitions or subsidiaries that pursue new approaches, task forces, and "skunk works" where new products and methods are allowed to ferment before they are reported to the large organization.

CONCLUSION

Although high market share usually leads to increased profits, critics often argue that high profits can be achieved with low market share too. They also suggest that firms with both low and high market shares show greater profitability than those that fall in mid-range because large firms with high market share achieve economies of scale, while small firms specializing in a given market achieve higher profits through "niche marketing." Medium-sized firms with neither of these advantages end with low profit margins. Thus, IBM, with 70 percent of the market share in mainframe computers, earns higher profits than Unisys, which has only 12 percent of the market. A. T. Cross Pen Company, through its 70 percent market share in the specialty pen industry, earns high profits because of its niche marketing.

Must market share objectives be followed by all firms? As stated earlier, firms that possess a large segment of their served market are better able to enjoy cost savings in production, marketing, finance, and other areas. This includes niche marketers like the Topol toothpaste manufacturer who pursues a smaller segment of a large market for toothpastes. But, when Pearl, K-Mart, and others began to market their own brands of smokers' toothpaste, Topol's profits suffered. While market share strategy is an attractive and desirable proposition for U.S. companies to pursue, it should be clearly understood that market share goals should be interpreted in the global market context to be practical.

CHAPTER 5

Total Quality Marketing: A Sound Solution

This chapter introduces Total Quality Marketing, a market-driven concept. It is different from the production-oriented Total Quality Management (TQM) concept. Perfect products do not sell themselves without proper marketing effort. Unless customers "perceive" quality, improving the product quality alone is not enough. Market Perceived Quality is also discussed here.

To make consumers perceive quality in a proper light, the application of TQMkt is necessary. Product quality by itself does not sell products, and improving it without regard to the marketability of the product is inconsequential. Therefore, firms should manufacture and market products that consumers perceive as good quality and value.

Business history is filled with examples of products that have failed miserably in the marketplace because consumers perceived their quality to be either inappropriate or inadequate. For example, New Coke, Listerine toothpaste, and RCA video disc are all products that failed in the marketplace. Another example is the unchanging negative public perception of American cars although American car makers made massive quality improvements to their cars. Cars imported from Japan or Germany in particular are perceived to be superior to the domestic makes.

The term *quality* means different things to different people. It has many meanings depending on whose perspective is used—the manufacturer's or the consumer's. For a manufacturer, quality means the most effective way of producing a product—saving time and money. For a consumer, it means that the product is "the best value" that money could buy.

TOTAL QUALITY MARKETING DEFINED

Total Quality Marketing implies using quality-integrated marketing-mix strategies. It is an enhanced version of the familiar four Ps paradigm of the marketing-management strategy—product, place, promotion, and price mix. By observing high quality in carrying out the marketing mix strategies, firms can improve the MPQ of their products. Naturally, when perceptions turn favorable, firms have fewer problems selling their products. Thus as highlighted later, TQM is equal to enhanced marketing mix. Its application leads to improved MPQ. Successful firms should aim for this.

Total Quality Marketing Paradigm

As shown in Figure 5.1, TQMkt goes much beyond product quality, which is the main concern of TQM. TQMkt is more comprehensive. Product quality is a necessary condition but not sufficient to propel the product to succeed in the marketplace. It covers not only the product and product quality aspects but also the promotion, price, and distribution aspects. Application of TQMkt should lead to improved MPQ that in turn produces greater customer satisfaction. Satisfied customers usually become loyal customers, enhancing the profitability of the firm.

McCarthy and Perrault (1993, pp. 598–604) maintain that firms should build quality into the marketing strategy application effort by doing as follows. Marketing strategy should define the blend of marketing mix elements that will meet target customers' needs. Once that is done, the plan places time-based details in place, making the application of the strategy easy. The plan should also lay out what everyone in the organization should do to accomplish the objective of satisfying the customer and making a profit. In organizations that accept the marketing concept, everyone should work together to achieve these objectives. Unfortunately, this does not happen often enough. There are many different ways to improve the implementation of the four Ps' decision areas. With TQM, everyone in the organization must be concerned about quality throughout the firm to better serve the customers—not just pay lip service to "the marketing concept."

Many things can go wrong during the application stage. Even people with the best intentions sometimes lapse into a production-orientation approach. Through various business and financial pressures, firms often forget the customer satisfaction objective and pursue their own business goals. Therefore, though the marketing concept is a philosophy that ought to guide an entire firm, most marketers need to work to keep the implementation of TQMkt on target as well.

Figure 5.1
Total Quality Marketing Paradigm

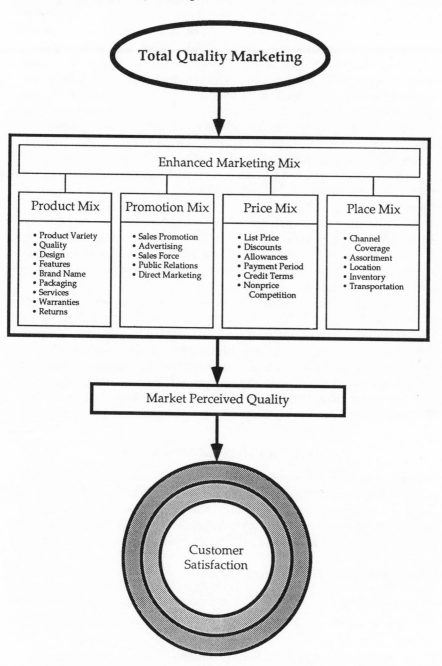

American firms today blindly believe TQM is a panacea, ignoring the quality of their marketing efforts. This attitude is dangerous. What they should do is manufacture products that have proper quality and market them at reasonable prices. For instance, there are more consumers for low-priced, good-quality cars than for high-priced, high-quality cars.

It is a mistake to think that all consumers want high quality or even the same quality. Most people are reluctant to pay the high prices that are usually associated with high quality. Also, as product life cycles become shorter because of rapidly changing technology, it is unnecessary to build excess quality into products that may become obsolete soon.

To a great extent, TQMkt and TQM show similar features in the product quality area. Therefore, it is important to understand these common features. Harvard Professor David Garvin identified eight different dimensions of quality: performance, features, reliability, conformance, durability, serviceability, aesthetics, and perceived quality aspects. Garvin also found several marketing-related correlates for quality: price, advertising, market share, cost, productivity, and profitability (Garvin 1988, pp. 49–50, 69–88). This classification enhances our depth of understanding of quality. However, further research is needed to find proper methods to measure MPQ.

In a market-driven economy, customer-perceived product quality is more important than manufacturer-perceived product quality. Therefore, manufacturers should pay special attention to consumer perceptions. Unfortunately, to most manufacturers, "conformance quality" is important, which means that their product has met stringent statistical quality control standards. On the other hand, for consumers quality is consistency in value and satisfaction—whether the product does what it is supposed to do.

QUALITY AS IT IS KNOWN TODAY

Today, quality has become synonymous with Total Quality Management. TQM has become a buzzword in American industry. To focus on TQM at the expense of ignoring marketing quality is risky. TQM is an operations management that strives to perfect the entire manufacturing process through improvements in quality and productivity (Daft 1991, p. 588).

One view of the TQM is as follows:

- Productivity gains are achieved through quality improvements.
- Quality is conformance to correctly defined requirements satisfying user needs.
- Quality is measured by continuous process/product improvement and user satisfaction.

- Quality is decided by product design and is achieved by effective process controls.
- Defects are prevented through process-control techniques.
- Quality is part of every function in all phases of the product life cycle.
- Management is responsible for quality.
- Supplier relationships are long-term and quality-oriented. (Cravens 1994, p. 417)

How Product Quality Became Neglected

Why has product quality been neglected by American firms? According to Michael Porter (1990), U.S. firms did not pay special attention to quality because of their lack of global competitiveness. The lure of huge defense contracts made many American firms more preoccupied with getting the contracts and completing them in time than with attending to manufacturing-quality issues.

After World War II, American industries were fortunate to be located in the only country that had an undamaged manufacturing base. The rest of the world's industrial complexes were either destroyed or became obsolete. Wartime pent-up demand provided American industries with a huge captive market where selling quantity through advertising was considered far more important than maintaining product quality. Industry's primary concern was to reduce production costs through economies of scale—not to improve product quality. Under these conditions, American firms flourished and created an illusion that the "Made in U.S.A." label would automatically sell products.

In addition, the reasons for the neglect of manufacturing quality can be classified into two broad categories: U.S. factors and foreign factors.

U.S. Factors

1. *Excessive concern for short-term profits.* Concern for short-term profits, even at the expense of product quality, has been the single major competitive weakness in American firms that foreign competitors exploit. Profits are no doubt important, but trying to make profits through manufacturing productivities alone is the wrong way. The right way is to see everything from the customer's viewpoint and then try to make and market products that maximize customer satisfaction. The giant retailer, Wal-Mart, found its way to success by marketing high-quality products at reasonable prices and offering many customer conveniences such as easy return, merchandising, quick inventory replacement, easy checkout counters, and the like. Because of these improvements, Wal-Mart's profits skyrocketed and it became the number one retailer in the United States.

2. *Neglect of "the marketing concept."* Although customer satisfaction is the focal point of the marketing concept, major concern in American industry has been to sell more products without proper concern for customer satisfaction. Such a callous attitude gave room to foreign producers who followed the tenets of the marketing concept seriously.

3. *Lack of consensus among labor, management, and government groups.* Inherent distrust between labor, management, and government is another major competitive weakness, making it difficult for U.S. firms to quickly retaliate to the threat of foreign competitors.

4. *High labor costs.* U.S. labor is among the costliest in the world. Labor costs have spiraled upward over time because of constant union negotiations for higher wages and more benefits, and of course increasing costs of health care, pension, and other retirement benefits.

5. *High compensation for top management.* Top management rewards itself with extravagant compensation packages that would make an Egyptian Pharaoh green with envy. Whereas in Japan and Europe the highest pay rarely exceeds a million dollars per year, many Fortune 500 company CEOs receive several million dollars as annual compensation.

6. *Investor concern for dividends.* Stockholders adore short-term dividends and stock appreciation. They show no enthusiasm for long-term financial needs of the firm such as new capital infusion to modernize plants, to retool machines, and to introduce robotics and other efficient management systems.

7. *Frequent hassles with government bureaucracy.* Various government agencies frequently interrupt businesses to verify infringement of any of the government rules and regulations.

In the above environment, marginal firms are unable to find funds for necessary growth and expansion. If a firm loses money for a few quarters to build market share, shareholders often get impatient, thus making it difficult for the firm to raise capital by issuing new stock. Therefore, some firms try to expand through mergers and acquisitions, finding that this is the only available option to grow. Unless manufacturing and marketing synergies are achieved, such actions generally exacerbate the financial problems of the firm rather than alleviating them.

Why are American businesses short-term oriented? It is mainly because profits are easy to quantify and serve as a measure of managerial competence. Market share gains are long term and quite difficult to measure precisely. Also, some companies would rather juggle corporate accounts and show profits to satisfy stockholders and vested interests. They often camouflage losses when possible by moving them to future years or transferring them to foreign subsidiaries.

Foreign Factors

Foreign firms have some unique advantages that American firms lack, including cheap labor, government support and subsidies, modern factories, the latest management methods, and better MPQ of products. Besides, Japan and Germany, tough competitors among all, had a strong desire to rebuild their economies after World War II quickly through global market penetration. Therefore, they try to grab market shares at any cost—even at the expense of some initial losses.

In addition, foreign firms do not operate under the profit pressure that pushes most American firms. Japanese companies, for example, are usually financed by institutional investors such as banks, insurance companies, and pension funds. Unlike individual investors, they can endure initial short-term losses while firms pursue long-term market share goals.

BENEFITS OF PRODUCT QUALITY

Product quality has several benefits. The following are the major benefits.

Increases Market Share

Quality helps build the market share. In the long run, focusing on quality protects a firm from losses because consumers often are loyal to quality products. Thus, even in difficult economic times, chances for survival are better for a firm that produces good quality products than for a firm that does not.

Reduces Production Costs

By decreasing waste in production, quality reduces production costs. Dr. H. J. Harrington, the board chair of the American Society for Quality Control, remarks as follows: "Historically we've said, 'Quality costs money,' while our competition overseas has been saying, 'Quality makes money.' And they've been proving it" (Harrington 1987, p. 2).

Increases Profits

Quality increases profits through increased customer satisfaction. High-quality products yield about 40 percent more ROI than low-quality products (Harrington 1987, p. 3).

Increases Productivity

Quality and productivity are closely related. Productivity is the ratio of inputs to outputs over a period. Systematic studies evaluating the relationship between quality and productivity have been rare. The few that exist have found a positive relationship between quality and productivity (Garvin 1988, p. 86). For example, a study of sources of productivity at factor level found that low levels of waste (scrap) were associated with higher total productivity (Hayes and Clark 1985). Another study that focused on productivity differences among various factories found that plants that paid greater attention to quality achieved higher levels of total productivity (Schmenner and Cook 1985, pp. 273–289).

According to Garvin, the relationship between the two is positive; especially when quality is viewed as conformance or reliability and productivity is measured as labor or total factor productivity (1988, p. 89). Thus the results of these studies vary according to the way quality is viewed or productivity is measured. Additional research is needed to establish more concrete relationships between quality and productivity.

IMPROVING PRODUCT QUALITY: A TEN-STEP APPROACH

After studying business practices of successful companies like AT&T, Hewlett-Packard, and others, Harrington suggested the following ten-step approach to quality improvement:

1. *Obtain top management support.* Without wholehearted support from top management, a quality program cannot succeed. Management should be willing to make heavy initial investments in plant modernization and new management systems, and they must support the program through its application stages.

2. *Establish a quality improvement steering council.* The specific purpose of this council is to include representatives from different fields of management. They should set priorities regarding where and when quality aspects must be carefully observed in production.

3. *Insist that all management people participate.* No quality program will succeed without wholehearted cooperation from all managers. Substantial education and training are necessary to accomplish the goals established.

4. *Secure team cooperation.* The team responsible for carrying out quality is to cooperate with others responsible for planning and managing quality programs.

5. *Obtain individual commitment.* Individual employees at all levels should be committed to achieving the firm's quality goals.

6. *Set up process control teams.* No quality program can be successful without periodic inspection, measurement, and control. Therefore, special teams must be established for this purpose. These teams should be thoroughly educated and trained on different aspects of quality. The training should also be continuous.

7. *Involve suppliers.* Suppliers play a major role here because the parts they supply must conform to the firm's specifications for quality. Even a small defective component can destroy a firm's general quality image. Achieving quality gains and sustaining such gains in many organizations are the result of as much of their procurement efficiency as of their production efficiency. Synchronizing these two key components becomes critical for achieving quality objectives in any organization.

8. *Establish a system to check quality levels.* Higher-than-necessary quality levels can hurt profits. Therefore, firms must establish a system to set appropriate quality standards based on selling price and other market considerations for the firm's different product categories.

9. *Develop and implement short- and long-range plans.* Quality must be observed in both short-term and long-range processes. In the long run, the firm must figure out different quality levels and methods of achieving these levels for all its products.

10. *Establish a recognition and reward system.* To provide incentives for those involved in the quality improvement program, management must develop reward and compensation methods based on aspects such as the extent of customer satisfaction achieved, the number of customer complaints, and so on. (Harrington 1987, pp. 11–15)

Such a quality improvement system would be a well-integrated comprehensive program. It would require cooperation not only from different internal groups in an organization but also from relevant external groups like suppliers.

Thus, first, it is important to recognize that most quality systems fail primarily because of lack of commitment to a particular system; second, a firm can develop its own system or adapt quality control systems developed by experts in the field; third, many systems are available that are developed by internationally known quality experts.

MARKET PERCEIVED QUALITY: THE BAROMETER

The barometer of the effectiveness of Total Quality Marketing is improved Market Perceived Quality. Products perceived favorably by consumers are likely to be bought by consumers in comparison with the products that are misperceived or not perceived well. Also, improved perception leads to brand loyalty among consumers toward a better-perceived product. Thus, the main objective of TQMkt should be to improve the MPQ of a product.

Market Perceived Quality Defined

The term *perceived* is derived from perception. Perception, a popular term in psychology, has widespread application in marketing—in consumer and buyer behavior. Therefore, the study of perception is important to marketers. To perceive means to see, to feel, or to view an object, situation, product, or service. Consumers tend to purchase products that fulfill both their functional and sociopsychological needs. Often, sociopsychological needs dominate, especially in affluent markets like the United States. For example, successful professionals buy luxury cars like the Mercedes and the BMW. On the other hand, the success of Ford's Mustang was based on the perception that the driver of that car projects youthfulness.

The Theory

MPQ relates to how the target market perceives a firm's product or service and depends on how consumers perceive a product or service quality compared to a similar competitive product or service. Because it acts as a measuring rod, a firm can estimate the effectiveness of its marketing quality depending on how consumers perceive its offering before and after implementation of a quality improvement plan.

A firm must make sure that its product or service meets the market expectations and is properly perceived by the target market as a prerequisite for their buying consideration. A product or service may have the highest manufactured quality, but it is of no use to the firm if customers do not perceive it as a superior product and purchase it. If the product does not fit the customers' needs as well as the competitors' products, the firm cannot sell the product to increase its market share.

MPQ is a combination of four independent terms: *market, perception, product,* and *quality*. These terms individually and collectively are as follows. A *market* refers to a wide range of segments that include prospects, suppliers, distributors, the public, and so on. Thus, the term relates to all categories of individuals and organizations that might directly or indirectly influence the behavior of consumers.

The term *product* includes both products and services. Tangible products consist of consumer and organizational products like office machines and computers. Though services are intangible, they need to be marketed like products. There are any number of product and service combinations.

Often, a *product* means a bundle of tangible and intangible benefits packaged together. According to Philip Kotler, there are three levels of product: the core product, the tangible product, and the augmented product. Core product consists of the actual physical product. Tangible product contains the following features: packaging, brand name, quality, styling, and features. Augmented product consists of installation, delivery and credit, and after-sale service (1988, p. 446). Thus an automobile purchase involves not only buying the actual vehicle (core product) but also its brand name and quality (tangible product) and delivery and service (augmented product). To succeed in a highly competitive world, manufacturers must excel in all three product levels.

How Does MPQ Work?

According to Shanklin, quality does pay (1989, pp. 42–43). Since 1972, the Profit Impact of Marketing Strategies (PIMS) program at the Strategic Planning Institute has collected and analyzed information contributed by 450 major companies. PIMS has found that no matter what measure of profitability is used, be it a return on sales or return on investment, profitability is strongly associated with product or service quality as perceived by customers. Companies that offer products and services of superior quality compared with that of the competition, capture customer loyalty and repeat business, exercise more control over price and market share gains, and lower costs of marketing.

PIMS figures out whether a company has a high, medium, or low market share by comparing the company's share with those of the three largest competitors. Companies with high market shares and high perceived product or service quality had an average return on investment (ROI) of 38 percent, compared with 20 percent for companies with high market share and low perceived product quality.

PIMS found that not only does high perceived quality allow a company to have greater control over price, it also has no effect on costs. So companies with high perceived product quality can charge higher prices to customers at costs comparable to those of their competitors.

Core Features of Perception

Perception. The study of perception is largely the study of what humans consciously or subconsciously add to or subtract from their raw sensory inputs to produce a private and selective picture of the world. Perception can be defined as the process whereby an individual selects, interprets, and organizes stimuli into a meaningful and coherent picture of the world. A stimulus is any unit of input to the senses—products, packages, brand names, advertisements, and commercials (Schiffman and Kanuk 1983, p. 136).

Perceptual Shield. In our message-cluttered society, it is difficult to make consumers perceive a firm's message. Consumers often set up a defensive barrier called the perceptual shield to protect themselves from unwanted messages. Marketers must break through this sensory barrier via effective promotional campaigns.

Perceptual Threshold. The lowest level at which an individual can experience a sensation is called the *absolute threshold*. Promotional messages that cannot break through this barrier are futile. For example, supermarket shoppers usually do not hear small noises while they are shopping. But they notice the crying of a child in the next aisle since the noise is loud enough to penetrate their perceptual threshold barrier. Similarly, when the cost of cocoa beans increases, chocolate-bar manufacturers decrease the size of chocolate bars without customers noticing the change. Small differences that can be detected between two stimuli are called the *differential threshold* or *just noticeable difference* (JND), a subject discussed at some length a little later.

Marketers should find out the JND for their products. Hyundai sets the price of its new Sonata model $2,000 below the prices of comparable cars—Ford Taurus, Toyota Camry, Mazda 626, and Honda Accord. In essence, marketers should aim to achieve two objectives: to penetrate target consumers' perceptual shields and to persuade them to differentiate the firm's products more positively than those of competitors.

Perception is selective. Consumers selectively choose stimuli they will perceive. Also, they usually see what they expect to see based on their familiarity, experience, and predisposition and block messages that are irrelevant or incongruent with their preexisting attitudinal frames (by zapping television commercials, for example).

Consumers hold different perceptions about the same product. Two individuals may perceive a product differently because of differences in their individual backgrounds—age, sex, economic status, social class, reference group influence, or the like. A product or brand that is liked by one person may be disliked by another person. Some people may not want to buy a BMW though they can afford it. On the other hand, young and ambitious professionals like doctors, lawyers, and businesspeople drive expensive cars to impress others.

Consumers tend to organize sensations or images into groups and perceive them as a whole rather than as detached segments. This process is known as the *Gestalt* process (*Gestalt* means pattern or shape). Its chief elements are the figure and group relationships, grouping, and closure. Therefore, advertisers must exercise care in developing the message so that the ground (e.g., background music) does not overwhelm the figure (message). People see things as a whole rather than seeing the pieces. Therefore, closure is necessary. Thus, a circle that has a section of its periphery missing is nevertheless seen as a whole. Winston cigarettes once advertised "Winston tastes good, like a cigarette should." In their subsequent advertisements they carried the message to "like a cigarette should."

Perceptual mapping is a process that enables marketers to decide how their products or brands are positioned in consumers' minds in relation to competitors' products. It also enables them to see positioning gaps or holes in the market that they must try to fill.

Perceived Quality

Quality is relative. What is important is how consumers perceive one product in relation to others. For consumers to like a product, they should regard that product as something superior to others in both objective and subjective (perceived) quality. Zeithaml defines quality as "superiority or excellence" (1988, p. 3) and makes the distinction between objective quality and perceived quality: objective quality is measurable and comparable to a standard, while perceived quality is derived from consumer judgment. It is important, then, to translate consumer perceptions of quality into objective and measurable quality standards (Larson 1989, p. 1).

It takes longer to rebuild a quality image than to destroy a good image. Nevertheless, by using aggressive marketing strategies, a firm can restore its positive image as exemplified by Johnson & Johnson's handling of the Tylenol poisoning case.

During the mid-1980s when some Tylenol capsules were found to contain poison, Johnson & Johnson immediately stopped production of capsules and urged retailers to remove all Tylenol capsules from the shelves. This self-initiated recall program cost the firm an estimated $100 million. In addition, the firm fully cooperated with the media to alert consumers and retailers and launched a crash program to develop safer packaging for capsules. Such an image of social responsibility allowed the firm to quickly regain 96 percent of its prior sales.

Reference Quality

The literature dealing with pricing problems and strategies reports considerable research on the idea of reference price. *Reference price* is the price consumers use to form their price perceptions of a product and to find whether a product is priced higher or lower. In other words, reference price provides a benchmark for comparison.

By analogy one can postulate that from a perceptual perspective consumers may use reference quality just as they may be using reference price. Reference quality may be defined as the quality level that consumers are likely to use as a benchmark for comparison in concluding that a given product is high, average, or low quality.

Such reference quality may change from time to time and from market segment to market segment. For example, reference quality levels in U.S. domestic markets are much higher than they were, say, a decade ago. Such reference quality takes place because of intense competitive environment. For example, one may surmise that reference quality levels of automobiles are much higher today than they were in the past. Such increases in reference quality levels can be attributed to better quality automobiles marketed by foreign automobile manufacturers, particularly the Japanese. As the reference quality levels keep increasing, even if U.S. manufacturers improve quality of their products, they may not be gaining competitively. This occurs because of the general upward shift in the expectations of reference quality among American consumers. This shift is taking place in many product markets both in the United States and abroad.

JUST NOTICEABLE DIFFERENCE (JND)

Successful firms put just enough quality in their products instead of giving either a low or a high quality for a given price. Finding out the exact quality that needs to be offered is more an art than a science.

However, firms with many years of experience in the business are better able to judge the exact amount of quality they must offer for their products. Anything less will turn consumers to competition. Giving more quality for the price will result in increased costs and reduced profits.

Discovered by Ernest Weber, a nineteenth-century German scientist, the JND between two stimuli is not an absolute amount but a proportion of the intensity of the first stimulus. The stronger the first stimulus, the greater the additional intensity required for the second stimulus to be perceived as different. Thus, despite significant quality improvements in their products, some firms might find it difficult to portray the JND of their products persuasively. To clearly differentiate their products from American makes, foreign automakers try to create attractive and better-product designs. They add more convenience features, offer better service, and sell at competitive prices, making it more difficult for American firms to create their own version of JND.

JND has many other uses as well. For example, retailers generally mark prices down by as much as 20 percent so that consumers notice the difference. Therefore, manufacturers and marketers try to use JND for their products for two very different reasons: (1) so that reductions in product size, increases in price, or changes in packaging are not readily discernible to the public, and (2) so that product improvements are readily discernible to the public without being too costly—to avoid losses from costly improvements that customers will not pay for (Schiffman and Kanuk 1983, p. 138). When judiciously used, JND can be a powerful marketing tool to augment MPQ.

In essence, MPQ depends on a firm's marketing mix. The shape of its response to an increase or decrease in a firm's marketing efforts is like an S curve (i.e., decreases are usually rapid downward rollercoaster rides, while the increases are slow).

MPQ is also quite sensitive to changes in the environment, often affected by adverse information like product recalls or bad publicity. For instance, sales of Tylenol dropped tremendously after people died because of taking pills laced with cyanide. Conversely, after being chosen as the *Motor Trend* car of the year, an automobile's sales might not increase rapidly as they would decrease in case of bad publicity. Therefore, well-managed firms like Johnson & Johnson will try to reduce potential damages to their image through continuous "intelligence monitoring" of the environment and by taking effective actions to reduce any damages. Soon after the Tylenol incident, Johnson & Johnson regained the market share by combining a public relations campaign with an effective quality-integrated marketing strategy.

To better manage MPQ, its relationships to market share, profits, customer value, sales growth, "positioning," price, perceived risk, and "the marketing concept" need to be examined.

Relation to Market Share

Gale and Buzzell contend that a product's Market Perceived Quality is a driving force that increases market share (1989, p. 6). They further argue that when superior quality and large market share are both present, profits are virtually guaranteed, changing the "competitive positioning" of the product.

To increase its aggregate market share, Honda introduced high-quality, high-priced Accura models through dealers different from those that handled its regular Honda models. Other Japanese automakers are now emulating Honda's example. Nissan is marketing its expensive Infiniti through separate and exclusive dealers. Toyota's Lexus is another example. The latter two cars are evaluated as the top two cars in the 1990 consumer satisfaction ratings. With these upgraded versions, Japanese auto makers are successfully competing with European auto makers like Mercedes Benz and BMW.

Relation to ROI

According to the PIMS data, businesses that have both larger share and better quality than their leading competitors earn ROIs that are dramatically higher than those of businesses with smaller shares and inferior quality.

Relation to Profitability

Businesses with a superior product clearly outperform those with inferior product quality. Several key benefits also accrue to businesses that offer superior perceived quality—increased brand loyalty, more repeat purchases, and an ability to charge higher prices. Quality shifts brand loyalties over time. Greater profitability of businesses with superior perceived quality is typically linked to their ability to realize higher prices while achieving lower production costs.

Relation to Customer Value

MPQ affects the way customers value a product. In most markets, there are three value positions: average, premium, and economy. Average value occurs when producers offer comparable quality at a comparable price (Mazda 686). Premium value occurs when a premium is charged for high quality (Mont Blanc pen or Mercedes Benz). Economy value happens when poorly made products are sold at a discount (BIC pen or Yugo car). When relative perceived quality and price are out of balance, a competitor adopts either a better-value position—superior quality at the same price or lower—or a worse-value position—inferior quality at the same price or higher.

Relation to Competitiveness

There are two basic ways to outperform competitors. One is to achieve superior MPQ by developing a set of product specifications and service standards that more closely meet customer needs. The other is to attain superior production conformance quality. Because these two ways are complementary, to be effective, they must simultaneously improve both MPQ and conformance quality.

Accomplishing a higher MPQ gives a firm three possibilities: (1) it can charge a higher price than before and keep profits; (2) it can reinvest profits in research and new product development to maintain the levels of quality attained; and (3) it can pass the savings on to customers without increasing price while offering a superior product or service.

Similarly, by realizing superior conformable quality, firms experience two benefits: A decrease in production costs and total costs and an ability to impress their customers with superior conformable quality that is valued by most customers and used as a key consideration in their purchase decision about the firm's products.

Relation to Growth

Quality is related not only to profitability but also to growth through its relationship to perceived value. Value depends on quality and price. Customers who receive a superior quality product at a low price receive a better value for their money—a "consumer surplus."

Consumers typically judge the value of a product by comparing it with that of the competitors' products. Though IBM arrived later into personal computers than Apple, it quickly gained a large market share because of its general reputation for quality, durability, and service in spite of prices higher than Apple's. It is perceived relative value of the total package of products and service that influences customer buying behavior and ensures competitive success.

Relation to Price

Divergent research information shows the price–quality relationship as follows: first, price and product quality are positively related (Monroe and Dodds 1988). Second, this positive relationship exists only under these conditions:

1. When consumers do not have sufficient information about product quality (Assael 1987).
2. When consumers lack enough product performance criteria (McConnell 1968).

3. When consumers lack experience with the product (Monroe 1976).
4. When consumers perceive high risk in buying the product (Venkataraman 1981).
5. When consumers perceive wide quality differences between brands (Lambert 1970).

Therefore, marketers cannot simply ignore consumers and set prices without substantial research. This would include testing and retesting price–quality relationships for products in various markets, at different periods, and under varied marketing circumstances. Marketers are better advised to consider the application of "reference quality" and "reference price" simultaneously.

Relation to Perceived Risk

Perceived risk plays a crucial role in purchasing decisions. Consumers perceive at least five types of purchase risks: (1) functional risk (performance), (2) physical risk (safety), (3) financial risk (cost), (4) social risk (shame), and (5) psychological risk (unhappiness). These risks vary for each consumer. Consumers try to reduce these risks by seeking more product information, by being brand or store loyal, by buying expensive brands in the product category (BMW or Mercedes Benz in automobiles), and by seeking reassurance from manufacturers (through guarantees and warranties). Quality will be inversely related to perceived risk. As consumers perceive higher quality in a product, the corresponding level of perceived risk will decline.

Perceived risk is also related to the country of origin of products traded in world markets. There is considerable research evidence that documents that country of origin influences perception of a product quality and perceived risk. For example, it is well known that before World War II and in the immediate post–World War II years American-made products were viewed as items of superior quality. In world markets today, however, many Japanese products are perceived to be of superior quality relative to their prices.

Such country-of-origin-related quality perceptions and the related levels of perceived risk are constantly shifting. Like Japan, Asian NICs have greatly improved consumers' perceptions of their quality and concurrently reduced perceived risk levels. Such country-of-origin-related quality perceptions and perceived risk levels equally apply to products manufactured and marketed by U.S. companies. In recent years, evidently, perceived quality levels are slipping and perceived risk levels are increasing for several United States–made products. This drift must be reversed if U.S. companies are to regain their competitive strength both at home and abroad.

Relation to "The Marketing Concept"

MPQ and "the marketing concept" are closely related. As Evans and Berman claim: "The marketing concept is a consumer-oriented, integrated, goal-oriented philosophy" (1988, pp. 10–12). The marketing concept serves as the overriding philosophy in conducting marketing management tasks of a company. This concept, which is presumed to be the philosophical orientation of American business, prescribes that management should strive to achieve company goals by delivering consumer satisfaction, which ultimately requires delivering consumer values at a reasonable and competitive price. Implicitly delivering consumer values entails delivering a quality product in a quality package with quality services that go along with the product. Such quality orientation should permeate both in the pre- and post-purchase phases of the consumer buying processes.

One may conclude that "quality" in all phases of marketing management practices is the key to successful application of the marketing concept. The successful global corporation of today uses "quality" as the cornerstone of the entire spectrum of its corporate marketing management practices. These aspects of quality-integrated, marketing-mix strategies are discussed in subsequent chapters.

MEASURING MPQ

A most challenging task for marketers is to be able to quantify highly qualitative (subjective) MPQ and use the information to maintain or improve quality levels. From the Strategic Planning Institute's (SPI) "quality profiling" process, we can develop useful approaches to improve the MPQ and to estimate payoffs. The five-step method is as follows:

1. A multifunctional team of managers and staff specialists first identifies non-price product and service attributes that affect customer buying decisions. For example, in buying office equipment, consumers look for features such as durability, maintenance costs, flexibility, credit terms, and appearance.

2. The management team then assigns "importance weights" to each attribute so that total weights add to 100. (For markets in which there are important segments with different importance weights, separate weights may be assigned to each segment.)

3. The team now rates its business unit's product line with those of leading competitors on each performance dimension identified in Step 1. From these ratings, a composite MPQ score is constructed.

4. Total MPQ score and other measures such as competitive position (relative price and market share) and financial performances (ROI, ROS, and IRR) are then verified against benchmarks based on identical businesses in similar

strategic positions. This is necessary to check the internal consistency of strategic and financial data and to confirm the business and market definition.

5. Finally, the team tests its plans and budgets for realism or practicality. Then it develops a blueprint for improving MPQ and to calibrate the financial payoff from such improvements. Often, the judgment ratings assigned by the management team are tested (and, when appropriate, modified) by obtaining ratings from customers via field interviews.

Difficulties in Achieving Consistency

Achieving a quality image and consistently maintaining it is difficult. Gale and Buzzell (1989) enumerate three major barriers that need to be overcome.

1. Competitive product differences often diminish as a market matures. Over time, imitators chip away the uniqueness originally enjoyed by a pioneer (Apple in microcomputers).
2. Complacency and failure to modernize a plant can damage relative quality (American automobile manufacturers).
3. Excessive cost cutting and misjudgment of customer preferences will reduce quality (Schlitz in beer manufacturing).

Finally, firms should be alert so that their products do not become generic products like Kleenex or Xerox or that competitor technology surpass them (videodisc could not compete with the videocassette player because the latter was an advanced technology product).

THE IMPROVEMENT PROCESS

Despite these stated difficulties, MPQ can be improved through periodic adjustments to a "relative value" that keeps changing as market conditions and competition alter. One way to improve MPQ is to adjust relative value is by adding extra value without changing price (nonprice competition).

Adding Value to Customers

Relative value can change for three reasons: (1) the firm can change what it usually offers to its customers, (2) customer preferences can change, and (3) competitors can change their product offering.

The first type of change requires an understanding of product and service attributes important to the purchase decision and a knowledge of customers' views of a firm's performance. The second requires gauging customer preferences through careful, frequent, and quality-directed field research. The third is seldom the focus of anything, the notion that quality and value depend on what competitors do being alien to most American managers. Yet, quality is the essence of the competitive aspect of value.

Nonprice Competition

Many companies neglect nonprice competition. They attempt to understand only how consumers evaluate one product against another. Businesses concentrate only on price although price may be the same for all competitors. Therefore, they never get to real nonprice competition cues and attributes that count in purchase decision. If customers care only about price, competitors preoccupy themselves with an endless spiral of cost-cutting and price-cutting strategies. Yet there is evidence to suggest that quality may be a more powerful and dangerous competitive weapon, even in price-sensitive markets where the basic product is standardized.

The key to this paradox lies in the effect of relative value on customer behavior. Businesses frequently achieve a superior total quality position by developing a better image than competitors or by providing better customer services than competitors. The PIMS studies show that businesses offering a broader product line and serving a greater variety of customers than competitors also score higher on perceived quality.

Finally, vertically integrated businesses offer superior quality on average. By controlling several stages in the production process, these integrated businesses can orchestrate various technologies and operations required to meet customers' needs more effectively than the competitors.

GENERIC STRATEGIES

Three generic strategies are available to improve MPQ: (1) catch up, (2) pull ahead, and (3) leapfrog. A catchup strategy occurs when firms emulate competitors by introducing "me-too" products. Its effectiveness is limited to reducing competitive disadvantage; the product looks similar to that of competitors without much differentiation.

In a pull-ahead strategy, products differ from the competitors'. By differentiating a product slightly (through JND for example), a firm could increase its competitive advantage. But this strategy is tougher than the me-too product strategy. Also, R&D costs increase because of developing additional product features.

Finally, the leapfrog strategy is more costly and riskier than the other methods. In a leapfrog strategy, a firm captures a big market share by introducing a new product (such as VCRs or laser printers) or a new distribution method (Swatch watches in sporting goods stores). Competitors cannot usually copy this strategy quickly.

Harvard Professor Michael Porter (1990) uses the word *differentiation* to represent the superior side of relative perceived quality. He mentions the concept of industry or market difference. Most of his examples describe a pull-ahead move where firms create better quality and market differentiation to command premium price.

By tracing the pull-ahead move through various segments of the served market, one can anticipate which customer groups and competitors will be affected and analyze how a competitor's pull-ahead, catchup, or leapfrog move would affect relative quality and degree of market differentiation in the served market.

CONCLUSION

In the quality contest, American firms must first recognize that a quality problem does exist in both areas of production and marketing. There are firms that plainly ignore this fact and continue to do business as usual as if there is no quality problem. Second, top management must be willing to commit and provide necessary resources to establish custom-made quality control systems that fit the firm's unique strengths and weaknesses. Third, firms must evaluate customer perceptions of product quality more frequently and take actions to rectify errors or manufacture and market new products without compromising profits at the expense of quality. Fourth, American firms must learn to set and follow long-term market share goals rather than short-term profit goals. Finally, American firms should regain market shares by using Total Quality Marketing along with Total Quality Management.

CHAPTER 6

Total Quality Marketing in Practice

This chapter reviews the ways firms practice Total Quality Marketing in different industries. The application of TQMkt in services, retailing, and direct marketing is also examined. There is also a discussion of who will win the quality contest.

HOW FIRMS APPLY TOTAL QUALITY MARKETING

Not all firms respond equally to foreign competition. This is how BMW, Cummins, and Motorola have responded to their competitors. By combining Total Quality Marketing and Total Quality Management together, these firms retained their market shares and thwarted further attacks on their shares of the market by other firms. There are lessons for others from the experiences of these firms.

BMW

Eberhard von Kuenheim, Chief Executive of the Munich-based Bavarian Motor Works (BMW) had to counter the challenge of Japanese automakers who began penetrating the market shares of luxury car makers like BMW with the Japanese made luxury models like Lexus, Infiniti, and Accura. These Japanese cars are beating BMW in the J. D. Power's rankings. According to Kuenheim, quality has a different meaning to different customer groups. For example, customers of McDonald's expect a quality hamburger. But customers of an expensive hotel like the Ritz in Paris may have a different concept of quality in mind. Similarly BMW customers, who pay up to $83,000 for a car, expect high-quality performance.

Kuenheim is fast adapting to the ideas of quality gurus like Japan's Genichi Taguchi and America's J.M. Juran. BMW shoots for continuous improvement. When Kuenheim became CEO in 1970, he gave the quality function "equal weight" with the powerful baronies of production and marketing. Now, BMW is dispersing the responsibility for quality throughout its organization. It can cut costs by undertaking rigorous audits of its suppliers. By scrutinizing the suppliers, the company has dropped several who did not measure up to its standards. The best dealers also are rewarded with higher margins. To build quality cars, BMW has built a $700-million Research & Engineering Center in Munich, where more than 5,000 engineers and designers work under one roof (*Business Week* 1991, p. 39).

Cummins Engine Company

Like many proud U.S. companies facing difficulties, Cummins Engine Company was an eager convert to the gospel of quality. In 1983, as the king of truck engineers reeled from recession and foreign competition, its executives made a pilgrimage to Japan. Back home, they installed a formal quality process. It didn't work. Problems soared on a new engine, warranty costs doubled from 1987 to 1989, and customers deserted. In 1993, the 72-year-old Columbus, Indiana, company turned a harsh spotlight on itself. It began to judge its performance using the criteria of the Malcolm Baldrige National Quality award. It even applied for the award, just to get reactions from Baldrige examiners.

It did not come close to winning, but the response prompted it to pinpoint the source of trucker complaints, to train workers better, and to seek help from quality leaders such as Xerox Corporation. Cummins now finds production defects in fewer than 1 percent of its engines, compared to 10 percent before these changes. Its warranty costs are down more than 20 percent since 1989. And in 1992, it emerged from three years of red ink. Using the Baldrige standards means a company must document, in about 75 data-filled pages, general statements such as the following:

- Top executives incorporate quality values into day-to-day management.
- Suppliers improve the quality of their products and services.
- Workers are trained in quality techniques and have a system in place to assure that products are of high quality.
- Products are as good as or better than those of the competitors.
- Customer needs and wants are being met and customer satisfaction ratings are as good as or better than competitors.
- The quality system holds concrete results, such as gains in market share and reduction in product-cycle time. (*Business Week* 1991, pp. 58–59)

Motorola

Chasing a quality award helped Motorola and NEC focus their goals. In the quest for quality, two trophies stand out: America's Baldrige award and the Deming prize from Japan. To win either prestigious award, companies must sweat through many hours and mind-numbing paperwork. Even losers have found that the wrenching self-examination, new policies, and tough standards needed merely to qualify for these prizes yield a valuable dividend. The exercise often transforms them into more thorough, more profitable, and simply better companies (*Business Week* 1991, pp. 60–61).

TOTAL QUALITY MARKETING
IN SERVICE INDUSTRIES

Quality in service industries is perhaps the most difficult to maintain. Firms can adopt certain new methods to bring quality to services marketing. Contrary to general perception, tangibilizing the intangible is the key to success in marketing services. Some researchers (Levitt 1981; Berry 1986; Berry and Parasuraman 1992) have expressed similar viewpoints. However, questions remain regarding what to tangibilize: should tangibilization focus on the actual service mix or should it develop a positioning strategy concretizing the corporate image? Clearly, the answer to this is situation specific, meaning it depends on each firm's unique circumstance. It must be noted, however, that it is usually much easier to tangibilize the image of a firm than its service components.

Unlike product marketers, service marketers have a limited choice of marketing strategies because of the intangible nature of the services. A better understanding of this difficult subject will help improve the strategic planning process of service marketing firms. "A service is any act or performance that one party can offer to another that is essentially intangible and does not result in the ownership of anything" (Kotler 1991, p. 455).

Services differ from products in many ways: they are intangible, perishable, lack consistency, and need participation of a service recipient to obtain them. These unique characteristics pose special challenges to service marketers. Marketers, therefore, need to be creative not only in developing new services but also in promoting, pricing, and distributing these services. More important is the need to clearly distinguish a firm's service offerings from those of its competitors.

To sustain competitive advantage, service firms need to clearly distinguish themselves from other firms in an industry and try to carve special niches in consumers' minds. This is market image positioning. Unless this is accomplished, any quantitative or qualitative improvements to existing service-quality levels will have only a limited impact on customers' perceptions of quality and value. This is especially true today because of strong competition and a variety of claims of various service providers. Under these demanding circumstances, to remain competitive, a service firm must tangibilize or concretize its image in the minds of its consumers. For example, McDonald's has followed a strategy of tangibilizing its image by promoting the golden arches symbol to represent the firm and by its consistent commitment to quality. Similarly, Prudential Insurance Company projects stability by promoting the "rock of Gibraltar" as its chosen symbol so that customers may strongly consider Prudential when they shop for insurance.

Another way to favorably dispose customers toward a firm is to improve the service quality and establish the image of the improved quality in customers' minds. Until customers perceive such improvements favorably, no amount of marketing the services will yield positive results. Several researchers have emphasized the difference between objective quality and perceived quality (Dodds and Monroe 1985; Holbrook and Korfman 1985; Monroe and Krishnan 1985). Objective quality is a term used to describe the actual technical superiority or excellence of the products (Monroe and Krishnan 1985) or measurable and verifiable superiority on some predetermined ideal standard (Zeithaml 1988). On the contrary, perceived quality has been defined as a consumer's judgment about the superiority or excellence of a product.

The most extensive research into service quality is strongly user based. We shall from now on use service quality to imply perceived service quality. Focus group research (Zeithaml, Parasuraman, and Berry 1990), identified ten criteria used by consumers in evaluating service quality. As enumerated by these authors, the criteria are credibility, security, access, communication, understanding the customer, tangibles, reliability, responsiveness, competence, and courtesy. In subsequent research, Parasuraman, Zeithaml, and Berry (1991) found a high degree of correlation between several of these variables and consolidated them into five broad dimensions:

1. Tangibles (appearance of physical elements)
2. Reliability (dependable, accurate performance)
3. Responsiveness (promptness and helpfulness)
4. Assurance (competence, courtesy, credibility, and security)
5. Sympathy (easy access, good communications, and customer understanding)

To measure customer satisfaction with different aspects of service quality, Parasuraman, Zeithaml, and Berry (1986) earlier developed a survey research instrument called SERVQUAL. As part of this notion, expectations are viewed as desires or wants of consumers (not as predictions of what will be provided). Subjects respond to a series of scales that measure their expectations of a particular company on a wide array of specific service characteristics. Subsequently, they are asked to record their perceptions of that company's performance on those same characteristics. When perceived performance ratings are lower than expectations, this is a sign of poor quality; the reverse suggests good quality (Lovelock 1991).

Here is an example of how a bank may try to tangibilize its service offerings:

1. The bank makes sure that its physical setting connotes quick and efficient service. Its exterior and interior have clean lines. The layout of the desks and the traffic flow are carefully planned. Customer waiting lines are not too long, and those waiting for a loan officer have plenty of seating. The background music reinforces the idea of efficient service.

   Physical surroundings can have a significant influence on both customer and employee behavior. In service organizations, the impact of physical surroundings is particularly important because it can decide the success or failure of a service organization's marketing programs. Many factors must be considered when designing a physical environment that enhances the quality of customer–employee interaction. These factors are ambient conditions such as lighting and temperature, spatial layout of furnishings and equipment, and the use of appropriately designed signs and symbols to express service concepts (Bitner, Booms, and Tetreault 1990; Bitner 1992).

2. The bank portrays a certain image of its employees. The bank's personnel are kept busy. They wear appropriate clothing. They are not dressed in blue jeans or other apparel that would create negative images about the personnel and service. Employees remember customers' names and use them during a transaction.

3. The bank's equipment such as computers, copying machines, fax machines, and desks appears modern.

4. The bank's letterheads and other communication material suggest efficiency. Pamphlets have clean lines without clutter. Photos are chosen carefully. Lending proposals are typed neatly.

5. The bank chooses an attractive name and symbol for its service.

6. The bank's pricing of its various services is always kept simple and clear.

7. The bank develops innovative packages for senior citizens and college students.

8. The bank offers a new telephone account checking service for the customers. Customers can find their account balances and transaction details through the telephone 24 hours a day.

9. The bank starts a new investment service by which customers can invest in stocks, bonds, and securities with no hassle and perhaps at discount prices.

10. The bank makes many ATMs available throughout the area to serve its customers.

Thus, the bank packages its service mix attractively to attract and retain customers. In the process, it also concretizes the bank's image through attractive symbols, atmosphere, and people well trained in communication skills.

Identifying Expected Service Quality

Before launching a tangibilization program, a firm should identify customer expectations regarding the desired service quality. There is usually a tradeoff between a perfectly ideal service level and the costs involved in providing high levels of service. For example, to give exemplary treatment to a patient in the hospital can be very expensive and sometimes impossible because of the lack of equipment or skilled personnel. On the other hand, offering marginal or submarginal service perpetuates a negative image that can ruin the chances of success for the firm. Parasuraman, Zeithaml, and Berry (1991) argue that the key to providing superior service is understanding and responding to customer expectations. The service provider needs to identify target customers' expectations of service quality. Service quality is harder to define and measure than product quality. It is more difficult to agree on the quality of a haircut than to assess the quality of a hair dryer. Yet customers make service quality judgments, and customer expectations must be known before service providers design effective services. Berry, Conant, and Parasuraman (1991) suggest a service-marketing audit to discover the strengths and weaknesses of the firm in the customer expectations of the quality.

Customers are satisfied by when, where, and how their expectations are fulfilled. Service providers must identify target customers' expectations with respect to each specific service. Bank customers' expectations of a trip to a bank, for example, may consist of no more than five minutes waiting in line and finding courteous, knowledgeable, and accurate tellers.

Consistent Service Quality

Beyond the concretizing efforts, service marketers must also make sure that service quality is consistent. Without this, the image developed after a long and strenuous effort can easily be wiped out. McDonald's (fast food) and Marriott (hotel service) are notable examples of consistency in their performance that helps them greatly in their image building. Some American firms, such as Delta Airlines, Hertz Rental Car Agency, H&R Block, and Federal Express, are also known for their consistence in quality. Other firms need to learn from their experience that maintaining consistency in service quality is critical.

Consistency in service quality is paramount to maintaining the "tangibilized positioning" (Lovelock 1991, p. 31). Once a positive image is created in customers' minds, maintenance of that image is crucial to the firm's success. Delivery of consistent quality differentiates a firm's offering from that of a competitor. Meeting or exceeding the target customers' service and quality expectations is the key. Expectations are formed through experiential and vicarious learning, service-firm advertising, and other communications. Customers choose providers based on their expectations after receiving the service, and they compare the perceived service with the expected service. If the perceived service falls below the expected service, customers lose interest in the provider. If the perceived service meets or exceeds their expectations, they are likely to use the provider again and build "brand" loyalty.

Thus, though "tangibilizing the intangible" is a key to success in services marketing, each firm differs from others in the manner it chooses to tangibilize—to tangibilize its service mix or the firm by itself. Some firms try to portray a physical object, like a piece of rock, as does Prudential Insurance Company. Despite the method selected, consistency in maintaining the quality is just as important. Once tangibilized, that image must be consistently maintained. Further research is needed to find out what kinds of images consumers would prefer for each type of service business, and it is important that these expectations be met.

The TQM approach helps everyone see and understand how his or her job affects what others do and how it affects a customer's satisfaction. Quality gurus like to say that a firm has only one job: to give customers exactly what they want, when they want it, and where they want it. Marketing managers too have been saying that for some time. But customer service is hard to carry out because the server is inseparable from the service. A person doing a specific service job may do one specific task correctly but still annoy the customer in a host of other ways. Customers will not be satisfied if employees are rude or inattentive—even if they "solve the customer's problem." There are two keys to improving the way people use quality service: (1) training and (2) empowerment (McCarthy and Perrault 1993, p. 602).

Firms that commit to customer satisfaction realize that all employees who have any contact with customers need training—many firms see 40 hours a year of training as a minimum. Simply showing customer-contact employees around the rest of the business so that they learn how their contribution fits into the total effort can be very effective. Good training usually includes role playing or handling different types of customer requests and problems. This is not just sales training. A rental car attendant who is rude when a customer is trying to return a car may leave the customer dissatisfied—even if the rental car was perfect. Thus, how employees treat a customer is as important as whether they do their tasks correctly.

Companies cannot afford an army of managers to inspect how each employee carries out a strategy—and such a system usually does not work anyway. Quality cannot be "inspected in." It must come from the people who do the service jobs. Firms that commit to service quality must therefore empower employees to satisfy customers' needs—give them the authority to correct problems without first checking with management. At a Guest Quarters hotel, for example, an empowered room-service employee knows it's OK to run across the street to buy the specific mineral water a guest requests. In the new Saturn car manufacturing plant, employees can stop the assembly line to correct a problem. At Upton's clothing stores, a sales clerk can adjust the price if there is a flaw in an item the customer wants.

TOTAL QUALITY MARKETING IN RETAILING

Different retailers use different approaches to adopt Total Quality Marketing. Here is the example of Wal-Mart, which seems to have really perfected the art of satisfying customers. Wal-Mart uses Just-in-Time (JIT) retailing to accomplish this objective. Even product manufacturers have lessons to learn from Wal-Mart's way of doing business. By using JIT retailing, Wal-Mart became the number one retailer, surpassing its arch rival K-Mart in sales and profits. In the following pages, how Wal-Mart does it is explained.

Whereas the Japanese are given credit for inventing the JIT methods in manufacturing, using JIT ideas in retailing is an American innovation (Reddy, Rao, and Vyas 1992, pp. 432–435). Using JIT ideas in purchasing merchandise, certain large retailers in particular can maximize profits and productivity. This section describes how JIT methods are used at Wal-Mart and discusses managerial implications for other retailers.

The JIT purchasing and inventory management idea was first developed in Japan to achieve manufacturing economies at Toyota Motors (Shingo 1982; *The Economist* 1987). To reduce growing inventories that often reach as high as 35 percent of total inventory value (Berkowitz, Kerin, Hartley, and Rudelius 1992, p. 425), JIT systems are now used by American firms (Frazier, Spekman, and O'Neal 1988). General Motors, for example, can reduce inventory costs by $2 billion in one year by adopting JIT methods (Kotler 1991, p. 204). Similarly, wholesalers, suppliers, and giant retailers like Wal-Mart and JC Penney are using JIT to enhance their competitive positions.

The JIT Concept

In manufacturing, JIT is essentially a management philosophy where the primary objective is to achieve zero or minimum levels of inventory (Frazier, Spekman, and O'Neal 1988; O'Grady 1988). Manufacturers buy raw materials delivered just in time to be used in production so that cash is not tied up in inventory. The benefits of JIT inventory management go beyond traditional inventory management methods that rely on the economic order quality (EOQ) model which specifies the order size that minimizes total costs of ordering and carrying inventory (Pride and Ferrell 1991, p. 409). The advantages include elimination of waste, enhanced product quality, improved employee morale and increased customer satisfaction (Inman 1991). Waste is reduced because the production goal is zero defects that mean less scrap and reworking. Product quality is enhanced for the same reason. Finally, employee morale is raised because there are fewer complaints from customers, who are more satisfied with products of high and consistent quality.

The principles behind JIT philosophy are simple. Excessive inventory covers a multitude of problems, enabling the manger to ignore them. The downside of this situation is that excessive inventory is very expensive. As inventory is reduced, problems become apparent, and managers are forced to solve them instead of ignoring them. Dealing with problems enhances organizational efficiency causing lower costs and improved service to customers (Schonberger 1992, p. 51).

Though it shares common philosophy with JIT in manufacturing, JIT retailing can be defined as the ability of a retailer to have just enough inventory for display and sale and minimal cash tied up in inventory in the pipeline. In retailing, another name for JIT is Quick Response Inventory System (QR), which is a cooperative effort between retailers and their suppliers aimed at reducing retail inventory while providing a merchandise supply that meets customer demand patterns (Evans and Berman 1992, p. 361).

Today, since buying sufficient merchandise and maintaining inventories at near zero levels are becoming critical to success in retailing, large retailers may have an advantage over smaller ones. First, large retailers are in a unique position to negotiate more favorable terms from suppliers because of their large-volume buying and long-term contracts.

Second, transportation and warehousing costs can be reduced by synchronizing delivery schedules with the retailer's needs and demand forecasts. Resultant savings can be passed on to customers as lower prices, making the firm's offerings more competitive.

Third, store shelves can be stocked with fresh merchandise since replacement orders are made at the point of purchase through electronic data exchange with suppliers, wholesalers, and manufacturers. This enables retailers to deliver goods at exactly the appropriate time.

Fourth, the JIT system enables retailers "zero customer feedback time." This means that as inventory moves through the system retailers can find out which products are selling which are not and then delete the slow-moving items.

Requirements

The application of a JIT system requires that certain conditions be met. These are as follows:

Frequent and reliable delivery. This is critical to avoid unnecessary inventory buildup. Suppliers must meet retailer delivery schedules to avoid being dropped from the list of suppliers. Understandings and agreements must be negotiated with suppliers in advance and to the satisfaction of both parties.

Communication links with suppliers. Retailers must establish electronic data interchange (EDI) with suppliers and their manufacturers and wholesalers so they can order merchandise directly from suppliers. Establishing EDI links greatly simplifies and speeds up reorder processes. Consequently, this helps increase sales and reduce markdowns and inventory carrying costs by helping to speed the flow of information and merchandise (Evans and Berman 1992, p. 361).

Efficient coordination. It is important for suppliers to coordinate their delivery dates with retailer demand schedules so that retailers can set up their merchandise displays based on delivery dates instead of placing rush orders, which are disruptive to both supplier and retailers.

Close relations with major suppliers. According to the 80–20 rule, 80 percent of purchases originate from 20 percent of suppliers. Consequently, it is important to maintain close relationships with this group of suppliers.

Pitfalls

To achieve successful application, certain pitfalls must be avoided (Karmarkar 1989):

Failure to obtain top management commitment. It is impossible to carry out successful JIT systems in retailing without strong commitment and support from top management. Since it requires a total change in the way the firm operates, wholehearted support from management is crucial.

Inadequate employee education. Employees must thoroughly understand the idea, philosophy, and procedures of JIT. They must also be clear about their contributions and actions that could decide the success of failure of JIT systems.

Failure to educate vendors. Not all vendors will show an interest in a JIT system. It may not be advantageous to them since it may increase cost for them to satisfy buyers who demand deliveries "just in time." Therefore, an education program may be necessary to persuade new vendors to accept and participate in a firm's JIT system. One inducement here could be guarantee of repeat orders and long-term contracts.

Failure to view JIT as an ongoing process. JIT retailing is not a cureall for retailing problems. It is an idea that can improve competitive efficiency of a retailer. Nevertheless, any return on investment in JIT systems is more long term than short term since optimum results may not be realized until the system has been in place for some time.

Failure to design proper software. Coordinating delivery schedules with the firm's merchandise requirement is essential, and computer software that links with vendor computers is necessary to minimize delays and to improve accuracy.

Thus, firms considering adoption of JIT systems should first see whether they can meet the minimum conditions discussed here and avoid the pitfalls.

JIT Systems at Wal-Mart

Wal-Mart's retailing operations provide a good example of JIT retailing. It is no accident that Wal-Mart's seventeen-hundred stores or so never seem to run out of merchandise although the firm maintains inventories at near zero levels throughout its distribution network. It is an amazing feat of coordination—matching merchandise needs with physical distribution plans—considering the tremendous volume of business Wal-Mart does.

At Wal-Mart, JIT systems are called "stockless systems." These systems are designed to minimize inventory levels as suppliers deliver merchandise according to mutually agreed-upon delivery schedules. Employees who enthusiastically accept and make JIT work are rewarded with bonuses and recognitions, and suppliers that cooperate are awarded with lucrative orders and long-term commitments.

"Retail Link"

Wal-Mart recently started the "Retail Link" program that goes beyond mere electronic data sharing with suppliers. Under this program, vendors continuously receive a variety of information on sales trends and inventory levels. They also receive purchase orders so that they can re-supply merchandise on time. For example, a men's slacks manufacturer receives purchase orders directly via satellite link, enabling the firm to offer slacks in 64 sizes and various color combinations and have them delivered promptly even in peak seasons (*Business Week* 1987, p. 80).

At the store level, two types of purchase orders are used: warehouse orders and assembly orders. Warehouse orders are 80 percent of total orders placed by each store. They contain information such as merchandise item number, description, vendor name, stock number, unit cost, unit retail price, size, color, and markup. Merchandise is usually ordered by a hand-held electronic unit called a Telzon that can unload information to the mainframe computer at the distribution center.

About 20 percent of merchandise orders go directly to vendors. In preparing these orders, a floor associate incorporates lead time, which is the number of weeks it takes for ordered merchandise to arrive at the store. Two factors are used in this calculation: a two-week safety stock and a two-to-four-week ordering interval. The objective is to minimize unnecessary inventory buildup.

Two problems can occur with either of these orders: stockout or overstock. Stockout happens when sales increase while order size remains the same. Since customers cannot get the merchandise they need, they usually patronize a competitor's store, and sales may be lost. Overstock occurs when excess inventory is accumulated, increasing the firm's carrying costs. Both situations must be avoided if the firm expects to remain competitive.

The Automated Inventory Replenishment System (AIRS)

Wal-Mart's success largely depends on its complex but efficient Automated Inventory Replenishment System (AIRS). The purpose of this system is to reduce managerial decisions to a minimum and let the flow of merchandise throughout the distribution network be as automatic and smooth as possible. This is accomplished through efficient computer linkages between the firm and its distribution centers and suppliers. Suppliers are continuously kept informed regarding merchandise needs.

The Distribution Center

The distribution center is the kingpin of AIRS and JIT retailing. By acting as a nerve center, it simplifies and ensures smooth flow of inventory coming from suppliers and going to various Wal-Mart stores. According to CEO Sam Walton (1986), the firm's rapid growth and profitability are due to its own version of "hub-and-spoke distribution" (*Marketing News* 1986). This is a system that enables management to take advantage of substantial quantity discounts in buying merchandise. Wal-Mart also first gives higher priority to location of its distribution centers than to location of its stores. This shows the importance given to logistics and efficient distribution by the firm over retail store location.

These distribution centers are strategically located and very large. They handle a huge volume of merchandise. For example, 205,000 cases of merchandise a day are unloaded at the rate of 13,400 cases per hour brought in by 190 trailers. On average, each center services about 150 stores within a 400-mile radius. Some 18 distribution centers service 1700 retail outlets nationwide; and storage space has grown from 11.8 million square feet to 14.6 million in a five-year period. Each distribution center carries about 8,000 items in stock worth $65.8 million.

Annual inventory turnover rate is over 15.8 times resulting in $1.74 billion in annual sales. The 98.9-percent in-stock rate covers 99 percent of demand. Finally, if the system breaks down, idle time cost is estimated at about $127 per minute. The costs include fixed costs, overhead costs, and opportunity costs of probable loss of customers to competition.

Therefore, it is important to keep the distribution centers working at peak performance level without interruptions.

Wal-Mart has other major advantages. These include superior management skills, accurate sales forecasting, and utilization of appropriate technologies to operate its distribution network. Most important, Wal-Mart displays superior management skills in coordinating employees and vendors to work in harmony to achieve common goals.

Marketing Strategy Implications

The adoption of JIT systems may not benefit all retailers in the same manner. Some retailers may not have the inclination to take advantage of the systems. Wal-Mart provides a good example of a retailer that incorporates the JIT system and benefits from it by saving inventory management costs and passing these savings to customers via prices.

Does a firm have to be as large as Wal-Mart to benefit from these systems? There are no clear-cut answers to these questions. Each retailer must decide whether switching to full or semi-JIT systems is worthwhile. Most small and medium-sized retailers, however, seem to prefer to do business in traditional ways since flexibility is critical in fashion merchandising and specialty retailing, and this flexibility may not be possible under the JIT system since orders are received and handled in a systematic manner that is less amenable to frequent changes.

Discount merchandisers like Wal-Mart are driving many smaller retailers out of business since the latter are unable to compete on price basis. Their inventory costs are usually high because they cannot obtain quantity discounts or achieve transportation economies.

Last, small retailers have two options: They can form cooperatives and try to obtain favorable terms from suppliers. It is ideal for these cooperatives to possess and operate distribution centers efficiently as Wal-Mart does. When they cannot adopt JIT systems, small retailers must consider adopting "positioning" and niche marketing strategies. Through these strategies, they can fill gaps in the marketplace that Wal-Mart and other large retailers are unable to satisfy.

TOTAL QUALITY MARKETING
IN DIRECT MARKETING

Quality in direct marketing can be said to be a wolf in sheep's clothing. It may appear that direct marketing is intended to sell absolute trash and has no quality, but the quality of direct marketing itself is surprisingly superb. Many retail marketers dismiss direct marketers as unsophisticated because of the tone and content of the junk mail they find in their mail boxes or the flashy jewelry they see on the QVC cable channel.

What they finally realize is that those "low-quality prestige" messages do not reflect a lack of sophistication of the direct marketer but surely are the result of highly sophisticated marketing systems. These direct marketing formats are consistently "low image" because this format increases sales and profits. One area of marketing that is fine tuned to its customer base is direct marketing.

Total Quality Control or Total Quality Management has been rising in popularity for a decade. Deming (1982) and Feigenbaum (1983) laid the foundation for building quality into each firm's production systems. To date there has been little academic pressure to apply TQM to marketing. Difficulties in accurately measuring reactions and attitudes are often cited as problems.

If one were to apply the principles of TQM to popular marketing practices today, the result would be to shift marketing efforts to formats consistent with what is presently called direct marketing.

What are the basic principles of TQM?

1. Designing for rapid feedback
2. Establishing control norms
3. Advanced statistical analysis of feedback
4. Rapid adjustment systems
5. Continuous feedback, analysis, and improvement
6. Customer orientation (Feigenbaum 1983, pp. 823–829)

Traditional marketers have designed their marketing systems as one-time product launches. Marketing research takes place outside the selling process on an ad hoc basis. Research is used to test the effectiveness of strategies. Tactics are developed to fit those research-based strategies.

Direct marketing, by definition, is interactive and controlled through databases. Direct marketing requires that a response or transaction at any location be recorded in a database. Therefore, direct marketing is an interactive system of marketing using one or more media to effect a measurable business response (Buier, Hoke, and Stone 1993, p. 5).

Direct Marketers as Masters of Continuous Improvement

Since the beginning of widespread direct mail marketing in the 1970s, direct marketers have used what is known as "testing against the control." Even when mail addressees were imprinted from metal plates, direct marketing used one "package" that had proven to be the most effective as the "control." Each time a mass mailing was sent, a statistically determined quantity of challengers (new proposed packages) was sent instead of the control. If one of the new efforts drew a better response than the control, it would be on its way to becoming the new control. In this manner, direct marketers have always kept close to their customers and been able to change with them.

Direct Marketers Know How to Segment

A regular marketer, asked who its market segment is, will typically respond with a good demographic profile. A direct marketer might well put out a multiple regression equation with over 50 variables (each variable on record for each prospect in their database) to predict the likelihood that any one name in their database will respond to a sales effort. The direct marketer solicits sales only from those members of the database who are likely to respond in such a way that the firm will gain a profit. Direct marketers may not understand why these people respond, but they know absolutely that they do respond.

Analysis of database response to test efforts has become highly sophisticated. Besides the most widely used multiple regression technique, direct marketers have been using discriminant, AID, and cluster analysis (Hichings 1987). The direct marketing techniques at present being adopted by various sales forces tend to find and sift prospects. Further, once these systems are in place, they tend to start feeding more information back to marketing than most traditional systems can handle (Silbaugh 1988).

Direct Marketing and Total Quality Marketing

Technology is providing us with increasingly more media, increasingly interactive, and the ability to capture and process huge amounts of data. This provides firms the opportunity to get and stay close to every customer. Traditional marketers prefer to deal with large market segments that can be treated in mass—mass advertising, mass production, and mass markets. Direct marketers, however, are increasingly alert to fine-tuning their efforts to each individual and developing a unique relationship with each customer. This is being accomplished through basic principles developed in TQM.

WHO WILL WIN THE QUALITY CONTEST?

The extent to which American firms will win the quality contest depends on the public's perception of American firms' competence to produce and market high-quality products. Unfortunately, past neglect of product quality haunts many American firms by creating a mixed image of the quality of American-made products. This makes it difficult for many people to believe that most American products today are better made than before. The problem gets accentuated if a low-quality high-priced product is marketed carelessly with a poor quality marketing mix.

In some LDCs like India, public opinion of products or services made in those countries is so poor that it affects the sales of domestic-made products. It is important to frequently evaluate the American public's perceptions of products made in the U.S.A. Empirical evidence suggests that public satisfaction with American-made goods was high not too long ago. According to one report:

More than eight in ten Americans (85%) say they are satisfied with manufactured goods. A third of all Americans (33%) say they are very satisfied, while half (52%) say they are somewhat satisfied. Only 10% say they are barely satisfied and 5% say they are dissatisfied. (Whirlpool Corporation 1983, p. 17)

Empirical studies also show that the American public is satisfied with the general quality of American-made goods and compare them favorably with those made overseas. A 1988 Gallup poll conducted by the American Society for Quality Control reported that

The perceptions of the quality of American made products remain at the same level as in 1985: 48% give American products high marks for quality compared to 51% in 1985, and two-thirds of the adult population feel that American made products better meet their standards of quality (up from 61% in 1985). However, an influential minority of 21 percent feel that foreign made products meet the quality standards better. (American Society for Quality Control 1988, p. v)

Thus, the American public has great confidence in the general quality of American-made products. Also, an overwhelming majority compare American-made products favorably with foreign-made ones. These reports clearly show that the quality contest is not yet lost. Overwhelming public confidence in American business should greatly help U.S. firms develop and carry out the new marketing strategies discussed earlier.

According to the 1983 Whirlpool report, for a vast majority of American consumers, the made-in-America symbol is an important indicator of quality. It was reported that 40 percent of survey respondents considered that made in America is always important as an indicator of quality; 24 percent said it is usually important; and another 21 percent said sometimes important. Only 15 percent said it is rarely important.

Simultaneously, American industry should also recognize that the public's faith in American businesses' ability to deliver quality is slowly eroding. Both the 1983 Whirlpool report and the 1988 Gallup Survey reported that there are significant intersegmental differences on quality perceptions. The Gallup Survey (1988) concluded that upper-income adults with greater disposable income differ markedly from the public.

Of those with annual household incomes of $40,000 or more, 40 percent favor foreign-made products or see no difference in quality. The strongest support for American-made products comes from older, poorer, and less-educated groups. These differences show up consistently.

From detailed data available in the reports, it may be concluded that better-educated and upper-income consumers, those employed in business and the professions, men, and younger adults are less likely to rate American-made products high in quality. From these segmental analyses of shifting quality-related American public opinions, two major conclusions can be drawn. First, more affluent segments of the American market, who will also be more discriminating consumers, are becoming more disenchanted with the quality of American products, and therefore their patronage may shift to foreign products if those are perceived to be of better quality at reasonable prices. This poses a serious competitive threat to manufacturers of products aimed at these affluent market segments. Unless American manufacturers reverse this trend, they will loose these markets to foreign suppliers at an accelerating rate in the future.

The second implication is that affluent segments of any society are usually "opinion leaders." Eventually, changing attitudes in these opinion leaders are likely to spread to lower echelons of society.

Interproduct Differences

Quality perceptions are not uniform. There are significant variations across products. In some products, the public may perceive that the quality of American-made products has deteriorated whereas in others it may be very well satisfied. Such interproduct differences need to be recognized. The data in Table 6.1 provide such interproduct differences.

These data clearly show that public perception of quality deterioration is higher in some product categories than in others. In some categories, such as automobiles, quality deterioration perceptions reached alarming proportions. Almost two-thirds of the public considers that the quality of automobiles has deteriorated. This may partly explain the woes of the American automobile industry. If this trend is allowed to continue, the American public's confidence in the industry's ability to produce and market quality automobiles will be completely shattered, which in turn will give competitive advantage to imported automobiles.

A further detailed analysis of such quality deterioration levels in terms of individual manufacturers and brands marketed can provide an index of comparative competitive strengths of companies and their brands. The other two product categories for which significant quality deterioration was reported are clothes and major household appliances. It is interesting that the least quality deterioration level is for home electron-

Table 6.1
Quality Improvement of Select Product Categories (In Percentages)

	Deteriorated	Improved	Status Quo
Automobiles	65	24	12
Major Household Appliances	30	39	72
Home Electronics	30	72	32
Clothes	34	26	40
Furniture and Equipment for Children	21	56	22
Small Household Appliances	22	37	41
Packaged and Processed Foods	15	48	37

Source: Whirlpool Corporation (1983), *The Whirlpool Report on Consumers in the Eighties: America's Search for Quality* (Benton Harbor, Mich.: The Corporation), pp. 29–30.

ics, an industry dominated by foreign-made goods. What can be done under these circumstances?

CONCLUSION

Why is it difficult for American managers to use MPQ strategy? One possible explanation is the problem of "unlearning." Quality experts like Deming, Juran, and others had stressed the importance of product quality for a long time. Now it has become a second nature for most American managers to think of product quality and ignore marketing quality.

Second, it is easier to measure whether zero defects are achieved in a manufacturing process while it is almost as difficult to measure the marketing quality in a sales transaction. The MPQ, which is based on a wide range of subjective customer needs and preferences, is difficult to measure.

Finally, companies have not yet developed a detailed guideline for evaluating MPQ under different marketing situations. Therefore, MPQ is a dynamic concept that keeps changing along with the market and competitive situations. A positive MPQ at once may become negative if competitors use catchup, pull ahead, and leapfrog strategies.

CHAPTER 7

Implementing Total Quality Marketing: Case Examples

This chapter discusses how some firms use TQMkt to succeed in the marketplace. There are lessons for others from these examples to improve marketing competitiveness of firms by putting "quality" into the marketing mix. Product, promotion, distribution, and pricing strategies are discussed. Integrating quality into the marketing mix means paying close attention to quality in all four Ps simultaneously to achieve synergy. America can regain its competitive edge with synergy (Corning and Corning 1986).

PRODUCT STRATEGIES

Improving product quality is very important. This can be achieved in several ways—through better design, by providing more free optional features, and through better pre- and postpurchase service, to mention a few.

Product Design

Durability. Durability is critical to product quality. "Quality is a virtue of the design." The durability or "robustness" of products is more a function of the design than of on-line control of the manufacturing processes. For customers, the proof of a product's quality is in its performance when it is used roughly. Therefore, robust products usually win customer satisfaction and, more important, customer loyalty. For example, customers prefer copiers that make clear copies in spite of low power and cars that steer safely on wet or bumpy roads (Taguchi and Clausing 1990, pp. 65–66).

Original designs. Some firms have outstanding reputations for design uniqueness and originality. For example, Herman Miller in furniture, Olivetti in office machines, and Bang & Olfusen in home stereo equipment created some good designs (Kotler 1988, p. 462). Today, many American firms lag behind their Japanese and European counterparts in creating original designs. Japanese camcorders, for instance, keep getting smaller and more compact each year, but their performance is improving and features are increasing simultaneously. In designing its Miata sports car, Mazda showed how a good-value product becomes an instant success in the marketplace.

Nevertheless, a satisfactory product design suitable to customer tastes is not always easy to create. A well designed product is functionally superior. Also, a good design should be aesthetically pleasing, safe to use, easy to service and repair, and economical to produce. It is unfortunate that most firms typically underinvest in developing good product design. It took major reawakening for some American firms to recognize the importance of design. General Motors' Cadillac division, for instance, hired an Italian designer to redesign its stodgy looking line. Similarly, Chrysler also hired Italian designers to improve the looks of its more expensive models.

Being original in product design has certain long-term benefits as well. One advantage is that the proprietary nature of patents prevents duplication by imitators. Thus, the patent laws insure that two Japanese Firms—Matsushita and Sony—own over 90 percent of the videocassette recorder (VCR) market. Matsushita's VHF models hold over 80 percent of the VCR market. Sony's Betamax holds about 10 to 15 percent of the market share. The remainder is divided among European firms like Phillips of Holland and Grundig of Germany. Matsushita markets its own brand names of Panasonic and National and licenses others. Thus, Matsushita licenses several Japanese (JVC, Sharp), American (RCA, Zenith), and Korean (Samsung, Goldstar) manufacturers' brands and makes private labels like Sears.

Consumer resistance to innovations is a major cause of the high rate of new product failure. Consumers resist new products because the new product threatens their status quo or conflicts with their existing lifestyle. Therefore, to launch successful product innovations, it is necessary to grasp the reasons behind resistance, including the usage and value barriers (Ram and Sheth 1989, pp. 5–14).

Emulate successful designs of others. Japanese automakers have successfully changed themselves from the world's worst designers to the best. Until 1970, Japanese automobiles—Datsun-Nissan, Subaru, Mazda, Honda, Toyota—looked rather unattractive in design. Since the 1980s, Japanese manufacturers have learned to streamline their cars with state-of-the art product design. Recent Toyota Camry, Nissan Maxima, Honda

Accord, and Mazda 626/929 models are good examples. Now the Korean automobile manufacturer Hyundai is emulating Japanese and German product designs. The Hyundai Excel, for example, is a duplicate of Mitsubishi's Precis. It is higher priced; Sonata imitates Mercedes Benz's models. Similarly, the Korean-made television sets and electronic appliances are mostly copycat versions of popular Japanese products.

It is ironic that the Japanese, who originally earned a reputation as copycats, are becoming good at creating original designs. Although initially they copied American and European product designs, today their product designs compare favorably to U.S. and European versions. The Japanese have also been successful in creating their own designs in electronics, cameras, and watches. Many Japanese automakers hire American design engineers and set up design engineering plants to develop and test new car designs that fit American consumers' tastes. Mazda, Nissan, and Subaru maintain product design facilities in California and Indiana.

Despite creating their own designs, Japanese automakers could not give up on copying successful products of others. Since Mercedes Benz is a leader in product design, several Japanese and American automobile firms copy Mercedes's styles. The Mazda 929 closely resembles the 1980 Mercedes Benz models. Some of Chrysler's sports cars are styled like the Toyota Celica. In turn, some earlier Celica models resemble even earlier Ford Mustangs. Toyota's Lexus 400 series bears a close resemblance to the Mercedes Benz 500 series.

Because product life cycles are getting shorter, creating original designs takes much more effort. It is much easier, cheaper, and quicker to copy others, especially if there is no violation of patent laws. Providing more and better user conveniences and attractive features in an automobile, for instance, includes the seemingly minor items that add extra convenience to customers. Thus Honda provides more leg room for the driver and driver-side passenger. Toyota claims trouble-free performance for its Corolla models. By pricing its Sonata at $2,000 less than the comparable Honda Accord, Toyota Camry, Mitsubishi Gallant, and Ford Taurus, Hyundai claims to give more product features for less money. Cruise control, power steering, power breaks, Michelin radial tires, a high-quality stereo system, a lifetime guarantee on paint, and the like are standard features of the Sonata.

"Bundle the Benefits"

Not too long ago, the auto industry used product unbundling. In an automobile, items such as radios, hub caps, floor mats, or full-size spare tires were not included with a new car. Customers were required to buy them separately. This unbundling was clearly intended to maximize profits by reducing costs. At present, most car manufacturers are "bundling the benefits" back in order to establish nonprice competition. European car makers like Volvo and Audi are following such patterns.

Unfortunately, American firms criticize successful Japanese and European product designs instead of emulating them. According to Cohen, "Instead of learning from Japan, the other industrial countries (prominently the U.S.) preferred to keep Japan on the defensive.... Respect for Japan's achievements are replaced by accusation of exploitation of cheap labor, government subsidies, dumping, rigged exchange rates, and most recently, industrial targeting" (1985, p. 134).

Enhance Durability

Highly durable products last longer in spite of heavy use. Nonprice competition is created by making products that are more durable than those of the competitors.

Historically, American firms have paid less attention to product durability since they preferred managed product obsolescence (i.e., to make products that would last only a few years). In this way, demand for new and replacement models is created. Automobiles are a good example of this. An automobile battery is usually built to last two to four years.

Trouble begins when customers get upset because batteries or other products "die" before or right after the warranty period ends. Though firms honor their warranties by replacement, exchange, or refund, the hassle of going through the process bothers many customers. Waiting at repair facilities and making trips to the shop all add to dissatisfaction. Dissatisfied customers create negative publicity through word of mouth.

Japanese firms have found that in the long run it is better to make products that last longer than to face warranty problems. Solving warranty problems requires additional staffing, trained mechanics, inventory, and paperwork. Also, dissatisfied customers can take a firm to court over a bad product. Such hassles can be avoided by making a higher-quality product in the first place.

Product quality is a more potent tool in increasing sales than advertising. It also increases customer loyalty. From the Japanese viewpoint, it pays to increase durability in their products.

American firms, on the other hand, cope with warranty problems by taking care of them as they occur. In the process, however, they do not seem to realize the disadvantages of selling a weaker product in the first place. Dealers may not like too many warranty problems; at least they do not lose money in servicing warranties because service costs are charged to the manufacturers. Unless American manufacturers strengthen product durability, warranty-related problems are not going to fade away.

Multiple Uses

A product that offers more benefits is more attractive to customers than a product that offers fewer benefits. Thus, a lawn mower that doubles as a snow-blower in winter is more attractive to consumers.

Manufacturers must discover new ways of improving their products or find new uses for them. Some firms give up on mature products, but the life cycles of mature products can be extended by finding new uses for them. Arm & Hammer baking soda company, for example, could increase its sales, market share, and profits by expanding the uses of baking soda; they market it as an odor fighter in the refrigerator, as a cleaning agent useful for miscellaneous household chores, and as a toothcleaner.

Ideas for new uses for a product can come from the firm's research, marketing, and production divisions; employees; channel members; customers; inventors; and the public. Discovering new uses and communicating the information to customers must be synchronized properly while keeping the competition in mind.

Find a "Competitive Edge"

Finding a "competitive edge" must always begin by finding out what customers really want. This means listening to them. Scripto introduced disposable pens that write well from any angle. People who use inexpensive pens get irritated when a pen does not write unless it is held in a downward angle on the paper. The U.S. market for disposable pens is over $400 million. If Scripto could capture 1 percent of the market because of its advantage, it would gain $4 million.

To develop a competitive edge that is sustainable is important. Competitors should be preempted from duplicating such points of difference. For example, Apple's Macintosh computer is designed so that it is impossible to copy. IBM's personal computer is regularly cloned by lower-cost computer producers from Japan, Korea, Taiwan, and Hong Kong.

Listen to Customers

Listening to customers involves frequent market research surveys, focus group studies, consumer panels, personal visits, hot lines, or even placement of computers with business customers or dealers so they can keep the company informed about new needs.

Cross-promotion by two noncompeting firms can sometimes be more effective in marketing products. For example, P&G and GM cross-promote their products. Most of P&G's customers are women, and GM wants to attract more women customers. P&G placed plastic car keys inside packages of Tide, Bounty paper towels, Charmin toilet paper, Folger's coffee, Crest toothpaste, Pampers diapers, and Downy fabric softener. If one of the plastic keys taken to a GM dealer is marked with a winning number, the winner gets a new Chevy Corsica, Beretta, or full-size pickup truck. P&G promoted Pepto-Bismol with H&R Block's tax preparation service by suggesting both of them as excellent alternatives to the stress of preparing tax returns by taxpayers themselves.

Modify Products

Japanese chain saw makers redesigned their chain saws so that the saws shut off if the oil level gets too low, a big benefit to new users who may forget to add oil in their enthusiasm to cut wood. This single design modification has given the Japanese the leading share of the rental chain saw market.

B. F. Goodrich has modified its vinyl wall covering so that it warns people of fires inside walls or in apartments below by giving off a harmless vapor that triggers common smoke alarms. Activated at temperatures below the ignition point of many common toxic-gas-producing materials, the product will prove difficult for the competition to copy.

Segment the Market Carefully

In the early 1980s, Coca-Cola sold two cola drinks: Coke and Tab. Today, the company markets New Coke, Coca-Cola Classic, Caffeine-free Coke, Diet Coke, Caffeine-free Diet Coke, Cherry Coke, Diet Cherry Coke, and Tab with or without calcium. These products come in cans, glass bottles, and plastic bottles for a total of at least 42 different permutations.

According to Kami, the consumer trend is toward

- Smaller families
- Desire for more leisure
- Better educated consumers
- Polarized (middle class is eroding)
- Highly segmented
- More skeptical
- Individualistic
- More female consumers
- More older consumers
- More impatient
- More insistent

- Informal
- Less brand loyal (1988, pp. 23–24)

Therefore, firms must segment the market; but they should not do it excessively. To tap the lucrative executive women's market, many urban hotels have separate floors for women. They also provide such services as fitness centers, hair salons, shoe repairs, travel agencies, and custom-fitting same-day-delivery garment services. Computer firms in trying to cater microcomputers to women, on the other hand, found the results disappointing.

Add "Value"

"Value" can be added to a product in many ways. Prepurchase or post-purchase methods of adding value are sometimes hard for rivals to match. These services include

- Trouble-free installations
- On-time deliveries
- Applications advice that is expert and timely
- Easy ordering systems
- Speedy complaint resolution
- Rapid responsiveness to technical inquiries that is competitive
- Excellent stocking of spare parts
- Competitive financing availability

Here are some examples of U.S. and Japanese firms that seem to do a good job in creating customer values:

Toyota's Lexus LS400. Lexus is a carefully engineered and well-designed car with the following features. It has a lower air drag coefficient than the Porsche 911. It economizes on gas at 23 miles per gallon compared to a gas-guzzling Mercedes Benz 420 SEL; Lexus is aiming for Mercedes's market. Its leather interior is made from a single cow's hide to prevent uneven fading. Recently, when it recalled cars to fix a minor problem, service personnel were sent to each customer's residence to pick up the car and return it after repair. These tactics increase the value and bolster the image of Lexus. In 1990, it ranked number one in customer satisfaction.

Steelcase Inc. Steelcase, a maker of office furniture systems, supplies its customers with 96.5 percent on-time deliveries of more than 12,000 separate product lines. No competitor can match this service value.

Snap-On Tool Corporation. The firm's tools cost two and a half times as much as its competition's, but the company dominates the mechanics' hand-tool market because it services mechanics better than its rivals and in more ways. For instance, Snap-On cleans every tool in its customers' tool chests every six months. Mechanics can also take eight to ten weeks to pay for new tools from Snap-On without interest penalties.

YKK Corporation. YKK, a Japanese firm, has become the world's largest zipper manufacturer by customizing zippers for individual companies and by selling customized equipment necessary to make zippers on line for its large accounts such as jean makers.

Digital Equipment Corporation. Digital customizes its office automation systems by client, only after providing a detailed assessment of a buyer's total network needs and documenting the required hardware and software to make it work.

Emulate the Master Copiers

Another avenue open for competition is to copy the master copiers. Americans, perhaps, have a great deal to learn from the Japanese, who are viewed as the world's most sophisticated marketers (Hall and Hall 1990, p. 135; Kotler 1988, p. 401). The Japanese are very good at marketing because they face intense competition in their home market, the second largest in the world (after the United States).

To succeed in Japan, a product must not only be unique but have very high quality and be adapted to the needs and preferences of very demanding Japanese customers. Most important, deliveries must be prompt, according to the tight scheduling of the Japanese. Only high-quality materials that are competitively priced and elegantly packaged have a chance. Japanese avoid any product that is presented in "economy packaging," and they dislike certain colors for certain products—yellow for cosmetics or toilet articles because they associate yellow with laundry or cleaning products.

The quality of their marketing mix has been the most important factor for Japanese success worldwide. Japanese firms have become experts in managing product pricing, distribution, and promotion strategies. Ironically, the Japanese have learned most of the modern marketing techniques from American management and marketing experts. Although the marketing concept—customer orientation—originated in the United States, Japanese became ardent followers of the concept while most American managers seem to fail to grasp the true meaning and implications of the idea.

PROMOTION STRATEGIES

In promotion—advertising, personal selling, sales promotion, publicity, and public relations—American firms usually excel. Although the Japanese have caught up and Dentsu is now the largest advertising agency in the world, the Japanese still use the best American advertising firms to develop and carry out their promotion and advertising campaigns.

Use Institutional Promotion

Judging from the frequent and numerous pages of institutional advertising in *Time, Fortune, Business Week,* and the like, the Japanese seem to know where to get the best publicity. Japanese firms (like American firms) spend millions of dollars on lobbying in Washington and the state capitals. Through their lobbying efforts, they gather information about potentially harmful legislation. They try either to prevent such legislation from being enacted or to reduce its effect on their products.

Japanese auto firms could increase voluntary quota limits from 1.6 million units a year to 2 million. Toshiba Corporation used extensive lobbying to alleviate pressures when Congress decided to punish them for selling technology that muffles the noise of Soviet submarines, making it difficult to detect them. Some Japanese firms are now funding research at American universities where they give cash funding or establish chair positions like M.I.T., Harvard, Columbia, U.C.L.A., and others, intending to benefit from the research.

Achieve Sales Productivity

Higher sales productivity can be achieved through sound recruiting, selecting, hiring, training, supervising, and compensating methods. Firms like IBM and Hewlett-Packard constantly improve their sales productivity by training more thoroughly, gathering competitive information, establishing realistic sales quotas, and giving their sales personnel full support, including laptop computers able to interact with production schedules. To achieve higher sales productivity, there should also be good teamwork between sales reps and sales managers. Sales productivity is a combination of talent and yield. Talent must be spotted, recruited, and signed by the firm. It then must yield high output thorugh training, targeting, motivation, and compensation.

Control Advertising

Today, advertising takes a back seat to promotion because of ever-increasing demands for better margins, promotion allowances, and the like from distributors. In 1976, promotion spending held at 57 percent, whereas advertising remained at 43 percent. By 1985, the disparity had increased—promotion spending at 66 percent and advertising at 34 percent (McGrath 1988, p. 126).

National brand manufacturers (because there is a lack of emphasis on national advertising to build brand images) are losing market shares to distribution chains like Wal-Mart, Sears, and Bloomingdale's. Sears Kenmore appliances outsell most manufacturers' brands.

Some retailers obtain consumer information more frequently. Data from sales checkouts are fed into computers for immediate analysis to find product or brand preferences by store, region, and country. Retailers can learn consumer preferences instantly, whereas manufacturers have to wait weeks or months for similar information.

Yet the problem of "battle of brands"—competition between retailers and manufacturers' brands—continues. The Limited, Wal-Mart, and Bloomingdale's represent brand image as much as any manufacturer's brand name. Manufacturers must invest more heavily in advertising to establish product awareness and distinctiveness.

Use Better Sales Promotions

Today, more firms are active in sports sponsorship as TV becomes a crowded advertising medium, and such major-event sponsorships offer highly visible, well-publicized exposure. Coupons are also becoming even more popular. Once limited to consumer products like instant coffee and peanut butter, they now are used for services also (airline travel, hotels, motels, photofinishing, dry cleaning). Instant on-pack tearoff coupons help makers of personal care products encourage brand switching right at the point of purchase.

Novel ways can be found to place a sample inside another firm's product package. For example, a new toothpaste can be sampled by wrapping it along with a bottle of mouthwash or shampoo, or even with a toothbrush. Refund offers are sales promotions used for autos, appliances, and so on. Refunds can help reduce buyer resistance to high ticket items. Without changing list price, a manufacturer or distributor can offer refunds for a period and then switch back to the original list price.

Contests raise awareness and sell more of certain brand names. McDonald's uses a variety of contests to woo customers. Although the logistics are complex (selection of price, number of winners, rules, duration of contest, delivery, and publicity for winners), a successful contest is worth the effort.

Some companies let customers help advertise their brands. Designers of clothing like Lacoste, Polo, and Calvin Klein have used their brands cleverly in ways that make their customers do their advertising for them. These firms send free samples of their products to celebrities (national, regional, or local) and get publicity when these celebrities wear them.

"Position" the Product Properly

In today's dynamic marketplace "product positioning" must be constantly monitored, evaluated, and modified. Johnson & Johnson enhanced market share of its baby shampoo by "repositioning" it as a family shampoo after discovering that many adults also use baby shampoo because of its mildness.

Through consistent quality maintenance, Japanese firms have transformed Japan from a poor, resourceless country into a rich and successful country. Consumers have developed a positive image of the country that transcends Japanese products.

Sabena Airlines developed a strategy to position Belgium (its home base) as a place to visit rather than simply a transit center for international passengers (Reis and Trout 1986, p. 138). American firms could also convey the image of "U.S.A." as a friendly country to trade with and to buy products "made in U.S.A." Emulating the successes of others and modifying existing product and promotion strategies are important in competing with foreign firms. Improve MPQ through positioning strategies.

The critical importance of Market Perceived Quality is emphasized in Chapter 5. It is also stated there that MPQ is not an absolute but a feature perceived in comparison with competition. Such competitively relative MPQ can be achieved through product positioning. Some consumer segments aspire to obtain high-quality goods but are either unwilling or financially unable to pay for them. These market segments emerge because of sociological and other lifestyle changes taking place in a given market. Under these circumstances, firms can design their product positioning strategies so that consumers feel that they are getting high-quality products as prestige brands but at lower prices. In this type of market opportunity, quality is more important than brand reputation.

Quality assurance is what makes consumers buy products although they are not prestige brands. In this sense, consumers will be willing to sacrifice prestige associated with well-known brand names if they can obtain quality products at lower prices. Creative marketers can create MPQ through their product positioning strategies. But practicing such strategies presupposes that manufacturers and marketers have first established their reputations as quality producers and marketers.

Japanese auto manufacturers seem to practice this type of "MPQ through product positioning" strategies. For example, once they established their reputation as quality auto producers and marketers in the lower-priced segments, they started developing and carrying out product positioning strategies to derive benefits of MPQ in other segments. Recently, they have been successful in introducing lower-priced sports cars to appeal to the changing lifestyles of certain segments in the U.S. market. Consumers in these segments cannot afford to buy really expensive and prestigious European sports cars, but their lifestyle orientation predisposes them to sports cars. Such a market opportunity was seized by Japanese auto markets when they successfully introduced several lower-priced sports cars based on their quality reputation.

Similar product positioning strategies to obtain MPQ were followed when Japanese auto makers started successfully marketing higher-priced autos in the prestige segment of the U.S. auto market. Obviously the critical variable that enables the manufacturers and marketers to successfully market their products is quality reputation. Once quality reputation is established, they probably can develop product positioning strategies combining the quality and price variables so that they can achieve competitive advantage through MPQ.

Carrying out strategy is usually just as important as formulating it (Shanklin 1989, p. 42). Ironically, it is nonmanagerial personnel—often some of the lowest-paid people in a firm—who carry out the firm's strategy and can therefore frustrate the firm's objective of giving maximum satisfaction to its customers. As far as the customer is concerned, the retail sales clerk, the manufacturer's representative, the flight attendant, or the telephone receptionist is the company. A manufacturer may offer the finest product of its kind, technically speaking, but this quality will mean nothing to a customer if a sales clerk is rude or a technician installs the product incorrectly. A company that spends millions on R&D and advertising may spend, by comparison, a pittance on training its frontline representatives on how to meet the customer. A poorly trained telephone receptionist alone can do untold damage to a company's quality image among its customers—or, more than likely, former customers.

A sign posted near one small-town retailer's cash register typifies the fundamental, people-oriented marketing philosophy responsible for the prosperity enjoyed by so many companies:

Why Customers Quit:
 1 Percent Die
 3 Percent Move Away
 5 Percent Other Friendships
 9 Percent Competitive Reasons
14 Percent Product Dissatisfaction
68 Percent Indifference Toward Customers

DISTRIBUTION STRATEGIES

Managing distribution has become more challenging and difficult as the role of distribution function in marketing has become increasingly complex. There are many ways manufacturers can distribute their products. They can distribute products through a single channel (automobiles), multiple channels (soap and toothpaste), selective channels (washers and dryers), and dual channels (books and shoes). Channel selection depends on product, market, and competitive characteristics of the industry.

This is an age of mass merchandising where giant retailers like Wal-Mart and K-Mart dominate as major links to consumers. These retailers have so much direct daily contact with customers that even big national-brand manufacturers like P&G are often forced to come to terms with them. These large retailers become the "channel captains" for most products they sell. They have an upper hand in negotiating terms and control manufacturers who want to sell products through them. To save costs, they use sophisticated methods like the just-in-time inventory management and direct computer links with supplier warehouses for automatic and quick supplies to their outlets. Wal-Mart, for example, passes distribution-cost savings to customers through lower prices than its competitors'. Thus, Wal-Mart makes it difficult for other retailers and factory outlets to compete with Wal-Mart and its associate stores like Sam's Wholesale Club.

Manufacturers make special packaging to sell through Wal-Mart's outlets. Some manufacturers become unhappy with their distributors and open their own factory outlets to complete distribution gaps for their products. In addition, direct marketing through catalog and cable television is growing in popularity in the 1990s.

Relationships with Distributors

Manufacturer and distributor relationships may not always be smooth. While manufacturers want better distribution with lower distributor margins and allowances, distributors want the opposite, like exclusive distribution and increased margins. Manufacturers do not want their distributors to control terms of distribution and delivery of supplies.

To control pricing and improve their quality image with consumers, some manufacturers limit the number of distributors. For example, many clothing manufacturers like Ralph Lauren sell only through selected outlets. Akai, maker of audio and video products, cut its American dealer network from 1200 to 150 to enable each of these key dealers to sustain the firm's quality image and increase profits on Akai brands.

Manufacturers like DuPont are forging closer links with distributors by using direct computer links with key resellers. DuPont is also funneling more of its suppliers' business through specified distributors who provide DuPont with just-in-time inventories and contracted-supply services.

Unable to find a suitable distributor, Mura, a Brazilian automobile battery manufacturer, bought shares in a small distributing firm in Florida to sell Mura batteries in U.S. markets. This is one way a foreign firm can avoid distribution barriers in the United States—a point to be well remembered by American firms unable to penetrate the Japanese and other foreign markets. Some American firms are also entering joint ventures with foreign firms to get their products distributed in foreign countries.

Multiple Channels

To add market coverage, some manufacturers use multiple distribution outlets—they sell not only through their own retail outlets or by mail order but also through large retailers, discount stores, and department stores.

Forward Integration

Many manufacturers have decided to integrate forward and own their channels of distribution. These include Tandy's Radio Shack, Sherwin Williams' paint stores, Hallmark's card shops, Hart Schaffner and Marx's men's clothing stores, and Bata's shoe stores.

Hallmark card company shows how one company successfully manages its distribution. Hallmark, the giant in greeting cards, markets over 32,000 different kinds of cards. Ninety percent of these cards are replaced with new designs each year. Over 11 million cards are sold per day via 65,000 outlets, most independently owned. The Hallmark distribution system interacts not just with marketing but with all other management functions from production to finance. And externally it must be reactive to changing customers, competitors, and environmental trends.

Manufacturers' direct outlets have certain disadvantages. First, capital is tied up in distribution because cash flow is required for operating expenses. Second, management can become unwieldy as the company must oversee both production and distribution. Third, when sales are slack (auto firms that own dealerships, for example), real operating problems occur because the manufacturers must worry not only about factory sales but also about retail sales. Fourth, when a manufacturer has its own distribution but also sells through normal channels (dual distribution), the latter may resent having to compete with manufacturer-owned outlets.

The results of manufacturer-owned retail outlets are mixed. IBM sold its retail product centers because of poor financial returns. Similarly, Hartmarx made more money manufacturing men's clothing than retailing them. An alternative to ownership is to franchise the stores. McDonald's owns 10 percent of its stores, with the rest franchised. Franchising allows manufacturers to control their market image, to obtain marketing data, and to gain benefits of entrepreneurial partnerships.

Novel Methods of Distribution

Just as with products, innovation in distribution is a key to success. Here are some examples. Japanese watchmakers achieved tremendous strides in improving their market shares by using multiple channels like discount stores, drugstores, and bookstores that the Swiss and American watchmakers had not thought about. Life Savers became a grand success when distributed through taverns and promoted as a candy to disguise a drinker's breath.

Aris Isotoner successfully sells its gloves from vending machines at sports complexes like racetracks. Abandoning its door-to-door selling, Fuller Brush began marketing its brushes at small kiosks in shopping malls. The Cable Value Network (CVN) sells a variety of goods to home shoppers around the clock. Factory outlets are springing up everywhere with a variety of manufacturer's direct clothing, kitchen appliances, shoes, jewelry, and toy outlets.

Creativity in channel design and maintenance can yield big dividends. It can generate market share at less cost, preempt competition, and build distribution arrangements into strategically advantageous operation. Understanding distribution realities, listening to resellers' genuine needs, and building flexibility into channel structures are ways to sell products to target customers. Without new distribution arrangements, a firm's growth opportunities can become limited. The key words are innovation and imagination. These ideas lead to new distribution methods, and growth opportunities can be greatly improved if they are used.

Foreign Trade Zones

Automobile manufacturers usually import 40 percent of their components from overseas sources (transmissions, engines, radios, etc.). To save on duties, these firms obtain a FTZ (Foreign Trade Zone) subzone status for their manufacturing plants. With this status, they greatly reduce duties, which are calculated and paid only when finished products (cars) leave the factory. Other manufacturers that import components should also use FTZs to reduce physical distribution costs.

PRICING STRATEGIES

Of all marketing-mix strategies, pricing is the most powerful and one that affects a firm's profit position immediately. In a billion-dollar industry, a 1 percent sales decrease means a sales loss of $10 million. At a 20 percent profit margin, the net loss amounts to $2 million. Therefore, pricing decisions must be made with utmost care.

Nonprice Competition

Nonprice competition occurs when a firm gives customers more for their money (high quality product, longer warranty period, and the like). A major advantage of nonprice competition is that it can be difficult for competitors to copy. Unlike price changes that are quickly known, nonprice competition features are not so easily identifiable. It is also difficult to figure out the costs involved in such nonprice competition measures. Nonprice competition can become an excellent and powerful weapon against competitors. Japanese automobile firms use nonprice competition heavily to attract customers away from U.S. car makers. Sometimes, firms may invest heavily in nonprice competition to combat competition and to regain market shares. For example, American car firms offer (for short periods of time) automatic transmissions, power steering, and air conditioning as standard features when competing with foreign firms.

Intangible Benefits

Customers buy packages of benefits that provide values. Price depends on values (or benefits), not costs. It is essential to group customers who value similar benefits and set different prices per segment based on these benefits. All pricing decisions are relative rather than absolute. Price changes can be easily matched by competitors, but benefits offered cannot be so easily matched. Here are some examples:

Procter & Gamble

P&G has bounced back to take the lead in disposable diapers because of their Ultra Pampers, a radically improved product with a superabsorbent polymer that turns into a gel when wet to keep liquid inside. P&G would not have captured 15 percent of the market with this new product if it had not advertised heavily in ways that dramatize the product's benefit. If tangible differences do not exist or are marginal, intangible differences such as customer benefits should be used.

Hanes

Hanes sells L'eggs pantyhose in supermarkets at lower prices than the higher-quality hose it sells in department stores. It obtains premium prices in department stores because of its skilled market segmentation.

Downy Fabric Softener

This product sells on the basis of intangibles—advertisement messages pointing out that users of Downy care more for their babies than nonusers.

Michelin Tires

Michelin tires sell at premium prices, and Michelin is positioned on the intangible premise that driving on Michelins will give customers a peace of mind and protect their families on the highway.

Charmin

Charmin toilet paper commands high prices than "no-name" brands because P&G differentiates its softness benefit.

Customer Price Sensitivities

Customers' price sensitivities vary depending on product needs and buyer knowledge. For example, when a product comprises an important part of the benefit sought, price sensitivity is bound to be high. Steel companies watch the price of coal closely since coal energy costs comprise a large part of total costs in steel making. Similarly, a homemaker making a cheesecake cares a lot about the price of cheese. When this is not so, price sensitivity is much lower. For example, manufacturers of suitcases are less concerned about the costs of sheet steel (less than 5 percent of luggage cost) than are steel desk manufacturers.

Price sensitivity is also lower when buyers have difficulty comparing prices. A peanut brand manufacturer, Home Brands, used this fact to its advantage. Its "Real" brand peanut butter is sold from refrigerated sections of supermarkets so price is more difficult to compare to that of other peanut butters sold in different parts of the store.

Price Battles with Large Firms

Pricing battles often occur as low-cost producers try to take too much share from industry leaders who react by lowering their prices to defend their turf. Industry leaders must try to avoid giving price discounts that are more than 25 or 30 percent greater than those of low-cost leaders since they are inviting their own end by encouraging some portion of their customer base to trade down their product or marketing requirements in favor of lower-cost substitutes.

In low-net-margin industries, cutting price is usually a road to disaster, despite volumes of new customers attracted. Between 1972 and 1974, A&P lost millions of dollars because it decided to market itself as low-price leader. A&P's campaign stating that A&P is a place to shop for economy was successful in increasing sales by $800 million on a base of $5.5 billion, but A&P's deficits surged over $100 million per year very quickly. In a low-margin business such as supermarket retailing, with its 1 to 2 percent margins, cutting prices across the board cannot increase sales volumes enough to offset margin shrinkage.

Textile makers who have tried to cut price to compete with imports have fared poorly for these same low-margin-structure reasons. Until they can differentiate their offerings or specialize by textile niche, they will be in trouble competing on price, since they do not have lowest manufacturing costs. Setting end-user price levels, communicating them, and revising them requires a great deal of finesse.

Price Innovative Products High

Innovative products should be aggressively priced. Kodak is betting that its small lithium batteries will have added benefits to justify higher prices. The batteries last 100 percent longer and will be priced 70 percent higher than the competitions' batteries.

The Japanese have taken a big chunk of market share in cameras, electronics, stereos, motorcycles, and other products by offering highly valued, well-made products at very reasonable prices. Manufacturers confronted with such competition frequently respond by cutting prices to try to hold share. The only response to meeting such formidable competition is to add valued benefits to offerings and compete on a non-price basis.

Competitor Prices

A best strategy in industries prone to price wars is to match competitor price changes in indirect ways. For example, when a regional competitive airline such as New York Air cuts fares on the busy Washington–New York route, Eastern Airlines avoided a price war by offering discount coupons on West Coast flights to passengers flying the other route. Many customers found it more advantageous to obtain these coupons than to fly on lower-cost New York Air flights. Discounts off complementary products are often used to avoid price wars. For example, to prevent a price war on film, firms will discount cameras or accessories they also manufacture.

Major foreign competitors use flexible pricing. For instance, Japanese companies do not blindly follow low-cost strategies. Instead of moving to standardization, they are shifting toward greater product variety to satisfy various market segments. They are taking a three-pronged approach:

1. Investing in flexible manufacturing systems, computer-aided design (CAD) and manufacturing, and robotics. These methods allow them to swiftly vary product features.

2. Distinguishing between scale-dependent product "core" and less dependent "periphery" enables Japanese firms to vary their product features almost infinitely without destroying scale benefits.

3. Obtaining intensive market knowledge and local marketing information makes it possible for Japanese companies to uniquely position products in different national markets and user segments.

CONCLUSION

Clearly, marketing quality must not be limited to product improvements alone. It must be integrated into a firm's pricing, promotion, and distribution strategies as well. Only then can a firm have a powerful set of marketing strategies working in its favor. American firms that plan to regain market shares must always recognize this fundamental fact of doing business in the 1990s and coordinate their marketing mix accordingly.

CHAPTER 8

Looking into the Future

As foreign competition continues to grow unabated threatening U.S. businesses, microsolutions developed and carried out at the firm level are no longer adequate to solve complex modern day business problems. Macromarketing must be combined with micromarketing to alleviate these problems. For instance, trade policy changes at macrolevel can take a long time to produce the desired results. Therefore, strategies at the individual firm level that emphasize building "market share" through improvements in Total Quality Marketing are very important. American managers today must adopt TQMkt to change the images of their products in the minds of consumers. Previously held notions must be replaced with a better Market Perceived Quality. These new strategies should be immediately carried out.

In containing foreign competition, American firms should work closely with government and labor to take appropriate actions. Unfortunately, cooperation among these three diverse groups rarely happens. For instance, in the controversy over the North American Free Trade Agreement, labor unions stood firmly against the government and big businesses, which both favored the agreement.

American firms must not lose the vigor to compete. The attitude "to compete" must permeate the firm always. Similarly, a commitment toward Total Quality Marketing must pervade the firm from top management to supervisory levels. Firms must develop and carry out effective marketing strategies to stop competitors from further challenging and attacking their market shares.

The import trade analysis in Chapter 2 shows that American firms have lost the leadership to imports in many product categories—from cars to cameras. In recent years, the Big Three U.S. automakers have slowed the erosion of their market shares through significant product quality improvements during the last ten years. To regain market share, however, the product quality improvements alone are not enough; they need to be included in TQMkt strategy.

It must be noted that in the twenty-first century there will be an enormous change in the way business is conducted globally. In such an environment, American firms cannot simply rely on old-fashioned approaches and ignore modern strategies. For instance, today global business no longer follows the Judaeo-Christian ethics that most Western businesses observe. Today, the religious bases for business ethics come not only from Christianity and Judaism but also from Islam, Buddhism, Shintoism, Confucianism, and Hinduism—and often from a mixture of all these. For instance, the core of Japanese business ethics comes from the ethics of Shintoism and Buddhism rather than Western business ethics.

Top management must be willing to commit funds and necessary resources to establish customized quality control systems that fit each firm's unique strengths and weaknesses. Second, under TQMkt, firms must evaluate the MPQ of their products and services more often and take quick actions to rectify their errors. Third, firms must learn to set long-term market share goals rather than rely on short-term profit goals.

Why is it difficult for American managers to use TQMkt strategy? One explanation attributes this to the problem of "unlearning." Quality gurus like Deming, Juran, Crosby, Feigenbaum, and others have stressed the importance of product quality for so long that it has become second nature for most American managers to focus on product quality and ignore marketing quality.

It is easier to measure product quality than marketing quality. It is easy to measure whether zero defects are achieved in a manufacturing process, but it is difficult to measure the marketing quality in a sales transaction. Therefore, the TQMkt, which is based on a wide range of customer needs and preferences that are subjective, is difficult to measure.

Companies have not yet developed detailed guidelines for evaluating the quality of their marketing programs. Market Perceived Quality varies under different marketing situations. Thus, it is a dynamic concept that keeps changing along with markets and competitive situations. A positive marketing quality can become negative if competitors use preemptive attacks or counterstrategies. Therefore, it is essential to conduct a SWOT analysis periodically to find out how a firm stands in comparison with its major competitors in terms of customer perceptions of marketing quality.

There is hope, however, for things to turn out positively for American firms. Congress might enact more favorable laws, or public sympathy could turn consumers toward American products. New technologies such as complete factories run by robots built with artificial intelligence may eliminate the advantages of low labor cost held by foreign competitors. American firms also may find new opportunities to trade with the former Soviet Union and the countries of East Europe, giving them the opportunity to catch up with foreign competitors.

Clearly, quality should not be limited to product improvements alone. Quality must be integrated into a firm's pricing, promotion, and distribution strategies as well. Only then can a firm have a powerful set of marketing strategies working in its favor. American firms challenged by foreign competitors must always recognize this fundamental fact and coordinate their marketing mix accordingly.

A careless advertising campaign, an unplanned pricing or distribution plan, or a weak product can easily put a firm behind its competitors for a long time. One cannot charge a high price for quality if the price is too far above the competitors'. Given these limitations, the basic question remains whether the American public is ready to pay a high price for better-quality products. If so, how much will they pay? These questions obviously depend on many variables and circumstances.

Selling separate service contracts has become common in recent years to provide fewer postpurchase services free of cost. Such contracts are generally disliked by American consumers. Although they may be willing to pay more for higher quality, they dislike paying extra for service. Why not build the product better in the first place instead of inconveniencing the customers?

Eventually, the proof of the effectiveness of TQMkt depends upon how American consumers perceive and react to quality improvement. Most important, would American consumers pay for these improvements? First, it needs to be established whether any of the strategies and tactics initiated by American businesses are perceived by the public as quality-enhancing measures. This is where Total Quality Marketing plays its role. Second, if manufacturers must charge higher prices or additional fees for quality-enhancing measures, it is necessary to test consumer reactions before such measures are carried out. Third, a detailed evaluation should be made of quality-enhancing measures from the perspectives of consumers. In sum, the attitudes, preferences, and satisfactions of consumers should be guideposts for developing and implementing the TQMkt.

CONCLUSION

Finally, the book focuses on the threat of foreign competition and discusses strategic approaches that American businesses should follow to regain market shares. Detailed discussion of the U.S. import trade is made. Attention is drawn to the importance of strategies based on marketing quality. The nature and dimensions of the concepts of TQMkt and MPQ are also discussed at length. The extent to which TQMkt is practiced in services, retailing, and direct marketing is also discussed. Like beauty seen in the eyes of the beholder, product quality improvements that are not perceived by consumers properly have no value. Last, an argument is made for putting quality into the marketing mix. All the four-P strategies—the promotion, pricing, product, and distribution—must be enhanced (i.e., carefully planned and executed). Periodic marketing audits must be conducted to identify trouble spots and rectify them.

APPENDIX A

Major Macroeconomic Issues

The purpose of this segment is to point out the major weak spots in the U.S. economy. These weak points accentuate the market share loss problem because foreign competitors take advantage of the U.S. weaknesses in penetrating its markets.

The two main problems—the federal deficit and trade deficits—are slowing the economy. If present trends continue, the growth of the U.S. industrial juggernaut could be seriously hampered. In 1988, this is what two experts had to say about the state of the economy:

> By any reasonable measure, the United States is growing poorer compared with many of its most potent competitors. While this reality can be cloaked in deficits and major devaluations, such devices cannot mask forever the fact that there has been and continues to be a full scale transfer of wealth from the United States to many other parts of the world. Indeed, these disguises only make the specter of the future more disturbing. (Levitt and Stewart 1988, p. 272)

Often a country's problems provide opportunities for others to exploit. The following sections list highlights of the economy's most pressing problems. The advantages of being debt free outweigh the disadvantages (Schuller and Dunn 1985).

Trade Debt

Since 1970, the United States has had a trade surplus only three times. Imports have been consistently on the rise, causing chronic trade deficits. Therefore, the most frequently cited symptom of declining U.S. competitiveness is the U.S. trade deficits (McCullough 1985). Furthermore, these deficits are the most visible manifestations of a much deeper set of U.S. economic problems: budget deficits, lagging productivity growth, low savings rates, and the lack of a well thought-out foreign trade policy.

The five countries with the largest deficits in 1988 were Japan, $52 billion; Taiwan, $13 billion; West Germany, $12 billion; Canada, $11 billion; and South Korea, $9 billion (U.S. Foreign Trade Highlights 1988, p. 62). Japan alone had an annual deficit averaging $50 billion until 1985 (Bergsten and Cline 1985, p. 2). And this trend continues into the 1990s.

Huge Public Debt

Another major problem is how to reduce the huge public debt. Despite the urgent need to reduce this debt, politicians do not risk making unpopular decisions—to cut spending on social programs or to raise revenues through taxes. The government is paralyzed by special interests and shortsightedness, which in turn make it incapable of responding to growing challenges.

High Cost of Economic Aid

Economic aid is given for different purposes: for physical infrastructure development, as relief for famines and earthquakes in different parts of the world, and as a creditor to the Third World and to the newly democratizing countries of the former Soviet Union. After World War II, the United States poured several billions of dollars into the war-devastated countries of Europe, Japan, and Southeast Asia to help reconstruct their war-torn economies. It is difficult to estimate the nonmilitary costs involved in liberating Panama or helping U.N. efforts in Somalia. Thus, the costs of these aid programs are a burden to the economy.

High Consumption and Low Saving Rates

Easy credit, the "buy now, pay later" plans, and favorable tax laws for credit spending until recently have boosted heavy consumer spending that in turn leads to increased imports. In addition, Americans save very little. The average savings rate of 4 percent in the United States pales in comparison to high saving rates in Asian countries. Because of a lack of savings, the United States must borrow foreign capital to sustain its economy and growth.

The Fluctuating U.S. Dollar

Only recently, the exchange value of the U.S. dollar is on the decline in international currency markets. In the last two decades, the high exchange value of the American dollar, compared with major international currencies, only helped to increase the flow of imports as imports get cheaper than American products. Efforts to reverse the trend (by lowering the exchange value) have not met with many successes. Though some increases were seen in American exports in 1988–1989, the increases in exports have not been substantial, and the imports continue to rise anyway. Relative price insensitivity of consumers and acceptance of lower margins by foreign producers have countered the effects of the falling value of the dollar.

ENVIRONMENT PROBLEMS

Lack of concern for product quality, long-term market share valued less than short-term profits, and the problems of low productivity are the major environment problems. Since foreign competitors do not have these major problems, they occasionally gain an upper hand over U.S. firms.

High Labor Cost

Labor costs are high in the United States, especially when the high costs of health care and pension programs are included. On the average, U.S. industrial workers earn three to four times more than their counterparts in Asian countries for comparable work. These high wage rates debilitate U.S. industry's cost competitiveness. For instance, because of low wages in Korea, the net imported cost of a Korean-made Hyundai can be $2,000 less than that of a comparable domestic model. This important labor-cost advantage enables foreign firms to sell their products at competitive prices. The labor costs continue to rise with rising health care costs and minimum wages.

Low Productivity Levels

The level of productivity rates in U.S. industries is comparatively lower than that of Japan, West Germany, England, and France. To increase productivity, American firms have introduced a variety of measures including plant modernization, retooling, robotics, worker and management training, and management techniques such as quality control circles and just-in-time inventory management. The net productivity improvements, however, have been less than expected.

Merger Mania

Mergers, acquisitions, leveraged buyouts (LBOs), and takeovers are not equally effective in producing societal benefits or adding synergies to help build competitiveness for U.S. business and the economy. Some of these actions are pure capital plays; some are simply moves in a game of self-aggrandizement. Many U.S. businesses and entrepreneurs—like Boone T. Pickens of Texas—play takeover games to make quick paper profits.

Poor Applied Technology

The United States is a leader in most fundamental scientific and technological innovations, including those fields that underlie computing and telecommunications, but it has often failed to translate this leadership into competitive products rapidly enough. Furthermore, the U.S. competitive position is declining because of the increasingly rapid rate of technology transfer in recent years (Krishna and Rao 1986, p. 47).

In product and process innovations vital for consistent success, U.S. businesses are losing their edge to Japan because traditionally less emphasis is placed on research in consumer goods and more on that in defense industries. The Japanese and other competitors, on the contrary, conduct extensive new-product research to develop and perfect consumer products, and they are constantly gaining ground on the United States.

Thus, from cars to computers, foreign competitors are edging out American firms in applied technology. U.S. firms need to match or better the foreign firms to be able to compete more effectively.

Lack of Consensus in Business, Government, and Labor

The lack of unity among U.S. business, labor, and government is clearly seen in the collapse of American Memories, Inc., a joint venture by American firms in response to the Japanese competition in computers. Traditional hostilities among labor, business, and government have not been helpful for developing a more focused trade policy for preventing the massive invasion of foreign competitors in U.S. markets. In Japan, for instance, there is tremendous cooperation among business, government, and labor to pursue common goals, and thus damaging intergroup conflicts are almost nil.

Better Management Methods of Foreign Competitors

American management and production methods were vogue until the 1970s. Since then, better methods are being used by foreign competitors, placing American firms at a competitive disadvantage. Most popular among these methods are the Japanese just-in-time inventory management, quality control circles, flexible manufacturing, and consensus decision making. Japanese firms operating in the United States—Nissan, Honda, and Toyota—also use these advanced management methods and achieve increased labor productivity rates and better quality control.

Protected Overseas Markets

Most lucrative world markets are closed to other countries by growing nationalism and protectionism. Many countries are leery of letting foreign goods enter their markets. Instead, they preserve their markets for their own industries to safeguard industrial employment or to conserve the outflow of their meager foreign-exchange reserves. To protect its own computer industry, for example, Brazil does not allow any foreign-made computers into the country. Similarly, India and other countries discourage imports of cars and other luxury products by imposing heavy tariffs. Japan, Korea, and Taiwan have a host of nontariff restrictions to bar foreign products from entering their markets. According to Waldman, despite advances made by GATT (General Agreement on Trade and Tariff) to reduce trade restrictions among countries, many nations are actually moving toward the managed trade. In this system, through direct intervention in trade and investment, governments try to better manage their own economies as well as the international economy (1986, p. 41). The Clinton administration is seriously working to crack down on tariff and nontariff barriers set up by major trading partners.

Preference for Short-Term Goals

Pursuing short-term profits at the expense of product quality and market share has become quite common with U.S. firms. The problem is endemic, caused by the cost of capital, the tax system, the pressure of financial markets, corporate incentive plans for executives, and the teachings of some business schools.

Thus, while the pressing problems of the economy and business environment engage the attention of the American government and businesses, foreign firms keep penetrating U.S. markets to enjoy the benefits of market shares and profits without having to share the burden of America's expenses or difficulties.

To sum up, it is obvious that the loss of market shares is caused by many complex factors. It is impossible to solve all these problems. But, being aware of them helps in minimizing their effects.

North American Free Trade Agreement (NAFTA): Beauty or the Beast

This section reviews details of the North American Free Trade Agreement and evaluates its merits in an increasing regionalizing trend in global trade. A successful NAFTA could increase market shares of U.S. firms in the global context.

In August 1992, the United States, Mexico, and Canada completed negotiations on the North American Free Trade Agreement. The agreement aims to remove tariff and nontariff trade barriers in goods and services and establish strong rules for the protection of investment and intellectual property rights as well. As a result, NAFTA will create the world's biggest and richest market with over 360 million people producing over $6 trillion in annual output.

The proponents of the agreement feel that trade will increase and that it will create a beneficial situation to all three participating countries. According to an estimate of the U.S. Department of Commerce, each $1 billion of trade creates over 20,000 jobs. As Mexico prospers, it will also provide a market for U.S. and Canadian goods, just as the United States will provide a market for Mexican goods.

MEXICO: MANAGING CHANGE

Mexico has been carrying out various economic and business reforms to make the country more suitable to forthcoming changes. If we consider Mexico as a corporation, it has made an enormous shift in its corporate culture during the last five years. A key to this change is the solidarity program.

Solidarity is a grassroots development initiative designed to improve the delivery of the basic goods and services to people in Mexico's neediest regions. It creates a way for small business communities to decide what is most important to them, whether it is potable water, electricity, or many other fundamental services. Thus, under solidarity the government provides funding, and the locals put sweat equity into developing the projects. This has been a remarkable agent for managing change in Mexico.

The change means setting the economic good for Mexico; the leadership has also announced a vital psychological goal—what Mexico really wants is to become a First World nation. In the past, the leadership in Mexico psychologically aligned itself with the developing nations and vigorously pursued protectionist trade practices. The psychological implications of striving to attain First World nation status creates a different mind-set.

In June 1993, the Mexican Congress passed a bill granting independence to the Central Bank. The measure creates a Board of Bank Governors with long, staggered terms. That largely removes the vital level of monetary policy from the hands of President Salina's successors. An independent Central Bank would imply that the next Mexican president will find it quite difficult to reverse the economic reforms currently in place. Another reform is in the formal law of nationality that required all corporations with any foreign ownership to obtain special permits from the Foreign Ministry. That could be a troublesome detail because of the bureaucracy. The new law helps the following changes:

- Waives the permit requirement
- Offers private investors 50-year operating concessions at state controlled seaports. This will reassure investors who were attracted to Mexico by continuity that NAFTA is expected to ensure in economic policy.
- Shows that Mexico's economic policies are on the right track. Attaining OECD membership would contribute toward making Mexico's market policies freer. Such actions have kept the exchange markets calm.
- Shows that Mexico's prudent economic management, which has achieved a budget surplus, could turn into a disaster if it is rejected.

NAFTA

Between January 1989 and June 1992, foreign investment in Mexico totaled a record $23.3 billion. The United States led all other countries with about 65 percent of foreign investment. Over the past couple of years, hundreds of U.S. mining companies have started exploring for minerals and metals—especially zinc, copper, and gold—in Mexico.

Getting NAFTA to this stage alone provides greater certainty that is very good for commerce and the movement of capital. NAFTA has also helped to alert Mexico to large foreign firms that previously did not include it in their planning strategies. Mexico, through its lobbying efforts, is trying to convince skeptical Americans that it has solved deficiencies and is managed by a "market-oriented" and open-minded people.

Proponents of NAFTA now have a high profile example to use when arguing that it can create jobs north of the Rio Grande too. In June 1993, General Motors announced that it plans to shift some production to Michigan from its plant in Mexico. The move could put 800 to 1000 laid-off employees back to work.

SYNERGY

The Mexico, Canada, and U.S. trade alliance has natural synergies beyond the regional proximity: Canada has vast land, lower population, and large natural resources. The United States has the world's most advanced technologies and a productive work force. Mexico has a temperate climate, natural resources, and cheap labor with enthusiasm to learn and improve productivity.

Mexico's other attractions are its demographics—only 4 percent of Mexico's population is over 65 years old, about 50 percent of its population is under 20. These numbers translate into major sales opportunities for the future; and if economic growth is higher than population growth, it means a continuous increase in purchasing power.

J. P. Gannon, Chair of General Electric de Mexico, suggested that the Mexican work force can do high-quality manufacturing. This is a result of rigorous training given to the work force in production and interpersonal communication skills. New concepts are embraced, people are empowered, work habits are improving; in short, change is occurring.

NAFTA may have other hidden benefits. Some U.S. companies may shift production from low-cost Asian locations to low-wage Mexican plants, generating new business for U.S.-based suppliers and capital goods manufacturers. Mexico and Canada are close to the United States. NAFTA will open opportunities for strategic alliances among U.S., Canadian, and Mexican companies. Medium-sized U.S. and Canadian companies with limited resources may look to Mexico as their first low-risk venture into international markets. If they can profit in Mexico, they will look for other opportunities around the world. It could be the first step in the globalization of North America's medium- and small-sized companies. Such moves will allow companies to put together different types of competitive advantages to make the whole region more competitive in the global arena. In short, to compete globally, what is needed is a large region with large synergistic resources.

Statistics confirm that the United States, Canada, and Mexico already complement each other economically to a remarkable degree. Canada and the United States exchange more merchandise than any other two national trading partners (over $176 billion in 1991). Mexico is America's third-largest trading partner, with $64.5 billion in goods moving between the two countries. Further, the trade among the three countries is generally in balance.

Several analysts compare NAFTA negotiations with the push in the 1980s for a single European market by the end of 1992. It sparked an investment boom in Europe in the late 1980s, long before the scheduled arrival of the single market. They believe NAFTA may produce a similar increase in investment in North America.

BALANCING COMPETING CONCERNS

The objective of NAFTA is to open markets. It is not designed to create a close regional trading block and does not build new barriers to nonparticipants. Despite the theoretical commitment to free trade and more open North American markets, trade ministers from Mexico, the United States and Canada have spent months in intense negotiations to craft a series of compromises to protect individual industries ranging from brooms to sneakers. The intent of these compromises would be to shield them from having to face a full force of competition too quickly. What the agreement consists of is a thrust of free trade, tempered by many protectionist details. Among the products protected by the fifteen-year phase out of tariffs are sneakers, ceramic tiles, household glassware, and a range of agricultural items such as orange juice concentrate, peanuts, broccoli, asparagus, and melons.

Rules of origin provide an incentive to use North American-made inputs. The rules of origin assure that the benefits of NAFTA accrue to the producers and workers of the three countries undertaking its obligations and that neither Mexico nor Canada is used by nonmember countries as an export platform to the United States.

Exclusion of labor mobility from NAFTA precludes any free movement of labor across the borders. Because NAFTA is a free trade agreement and not a blueprint for a common market, it does not require any change in U.S. immigration law. However, like the U.S.–Canada free trade agreement, NAFTA does contain provisions concerning temporary business travel allowing professionals to cross borders to provide services. This reduces the need for companies to move or set up operations outside the United States to service the Mexican or Canadian markets.

The most serious concern about NAFTA is its impact on the environment, labor (jobs), and adjustment issues when jobs are lost. AFL-CIO President Lane Kirkland has shown that labor unions might go along with the trade proposal if it improves the lot of U.S. workers, helps workers whose jobs go to Mexico, protects environmental standards in Mexico, and upholds standards for Mexican workers. Labor rights advocates are also calling for trade sanctions for labor violations in Mexico.

NAFTA AND THE JOBS

The main opposition to NAFTA stems from the fear that U.S. manufacturers will move jobs to Mexico where wages in some sectors are one-tenth of U.S. levels. This is a serious concern. The fact remains that industries in North America are in transition and will remain so for the next several years. This will cause hardship to workers who will lose jobs on both sides of the border. Trade economists have calculated that every $1 billion in U.S. exports generates about 25,000 new domestic jobs. Thus, exports to Mexico that amounted to $41 billion in 1992 translate into well over a million jobs in the United States.

The signing of NAFTA will result in a more rapid pace of job creation in all three countries. A publication by the Institute of International Economics (IIE), Washington, D.C., estimates that in 1995 NAFTA will create over 325,000 jobs in the United States while eliminating about 150,000 jobs—mostly unskilled and semiskilled factory jobs. This will be the result of some U.S. corporations moving south of the border to take advantage of the lower wages available from Mexico's unskilled workers. But economists argue that many of those companies would have relocated to the low-wage regions of the Far East anyway. They would have sought out new suppliers in these regions. By remaining on the North American continent, many of these transplanted operations will retain their U.S. suppliers.

There is a significant difference between the two options. The U.S. Commerce

Department reports that for every U.S. job supported by export to Mexico there are also two other jobs indirectly supported in industries supplying intermediate inputs and capital goods to those exporters. Although estimates of the exact number of new jobs created because of NAFTA should be viewed with caution, it is likely that the net increase in U.S. jobs will easily exceed 100,000 by 1996.

By comparison, Canada has lost 403,000 manufacturing jobs and gained 185,000 service jobs since signing the free trade agreement with the United States. After signing the U.S.-Canadian trade pact, Canada experienced a recession. A study by the Royal Bank of Canada and other respected sources has shown that the effect of the 1988 pact has softened the recession.

As competitive forces weed out the weak businesses, some jobs in both the United States and Mexico will be eliminated. Although the United States will lose some low-skilled jobs to Mexico, it will gain most high-paying, high-skilled jobs in export-oriented industries.

In Mexico, where some industries are not competitive because they were built to serve a Mexican market that was protected for four or five decades, industry will face highly efficient competition from the United States and Canada. Again, jobs will be lost, and some people in Mexico will be forced to move to other areas. For example, more than 1900 U.S. companies already have created some 453,000 Mexican jobs by moving assembly operations from the United States to Mexican plants known as maquiladoras (assembly industry).

Mexican adjustments, however, will not be painless. Some eight million Mexicans are unemployed, and more factories will probably be closed while others will be purchased and revamped by more efficient foreign competitors. For small and mid-sized companies, which make up 90 percent of all business in Mexico, fighting the competition and barriers at home such as interest rates of 25 percent and more is a severe hindrance.

In the retail sector, in the last few years many Mexican companies have either joined forces with American or Canadian companies or gone out of business. But Mexico's globally competitive multinationals like glass maker Vitro SA, cement maker CEMEX, and some 300 other big players are expected to increase their sales throughout North America, thereby creating additional employment in Mexico.

NAFTA does not necessarily mean that most manufacturing plants employing low-skilled or semiskilled workers will move to Mexico. The pact removes some Mexican requirements on U.S. plants that are already there to buy some Mexican components or to export most of their products rather than selling them in the Mexican market. NAFTA also ensures that U.S. plants operating subsidiaries in Mexico enjoy a "level playing field" with Mexican companies and with other foreign companies located there.

Mexican wages reflect Mexican productivity. Output per worker in the United States is five to six times that in Mexico. Since 1980, output per person employed in U.S. manufacturing has grown 2.5 times faster than that in Mexico. Total production and marketing costs are the keys to plant location decisions, not wages alone. If wages were all that mattered in the manufacturing world, the underdeveloped countries would all be economic powerhouses. A productive and well-trained work force, a developed infrastructure, a stable social and political environment, and easily accessible technology and capital are critical factors in the location decisions of companies. The United States provides all these, which mostly helps to offset the advantage of low wages elsewhere.

Lack of sophisticated transportation services in Mexico could replace trade barriers as the short-term impediment to fewer restrictive trade regulations. The Mexican infrastructure—the country's system of roads, bridges, telephones, railroads, airlines, airports, and computer linkups—is no match for that of the United States. For example, major rail lines into Mexico cannot handle the heaviest grain or chemical tank cars in use in the United States. Only 8.5 percent of Mexican highways are more than two lanes, and the country does not have a network of fuel supply depots or truck stops to smooth out logistic operations.

One final note on the impact of NAFTA on jobs. It is easier to point to a lost job than to show a created job. When an American factory worker says that he has lost a job to Taiwan, Japan, Korea, or Mexico because of a plant closing, it is easy to get media attention—and perhaps rightly so. It is difficult to point to another person and say his job was created because we did something more competitively in this region and much more difficult to get media attention for this success.

LABOR COOPERATION, SAFEGUARDS, AND WORKER ADJUSTMENT

The U.S. Department of Labor has negotiated a five-year Memorandum of Understanding (MOU) to strengthen bilateral cooperation with respect to occupational health and safety standards, child labor, labor statistics, worker rights, labor-management relations, and workplace training. Several joint MO initiatives are now under way.

NAFTA will also contain measures to ease the transition for import-sensitive U.S. industries, having a transition of up to 15 years for those sectors. In addition, NAFTA contains "safeguard" procedures that will allow the United States to reimpose tariffs upon injurious import surges.

NAFTA includes a new comprehensive worker-adjustment program called Advanced Skills Through Education and Training (ABETS). Under this worker-adjustment program, dislocated U.S. workers will receive timely, comprehensive, and effective services and retraining.

However well-intentioned, government assistance by itself will not make a smooth transition. Business must play a major role in providing leadership, setting an example to change, and investing heavily in training and in empowering the work force. A poorly performing worker may not be a bad worker, but a product of inadequate training and guidance.

NAFTA AND THE ENVIRONMENT

NAFTA allows the United States to maintain its stringent environmental, health, and safety standards. In February 1992, the EPA and its Mexican counterpart, Cytosol, completed a comprehensive plan for addressing air, soil, water, and hazardous waste problems in the border area. For their part, the Mexicans have made it clear that they have no intention of inviting investment in plants that do not comply with environmental standards set in Mexico's 1988 comprehensive law. Based on similar U.S. legislation, this law sets high standards for new industries. Since the passage of the 1988 law, the Mexican government has closed more than 1000 polluting companies, including Mexico's largest oil refinery in Mexico City. Mexico is also investing billions of dollars in a program to phase out leaded gasoline and to equip public service vehicles with catalytic converters. While much needs to be done, Mexico is on the right track to address the serious environmental issues.

If NAFTA is signed, it could be used as a leverage by the United States to ensure compliance by the Mexican authorities. Without NAFTA, there is no such control, and pollution in Mexico may get worse—the fear expressed by environmentalists who oppose NAFTA.

NAFTA will create prosperity in Mexico to fund the efforts to clean up their environment and enforce the tougher standards.

Officials in the natural gas industry are ebullient about the prospects opened by NAFTA. More U.S. investment in Mexico is likely in electric power plants, many of which will burn gas to reduce pollution. If NAFTA improves the Mexican economy and means more factories and plants there, then it should also mean more demand for U.S. gas and more jobs in the gas industry. U.S. environmental-engineering firms will also benefit. Their services are in great demand in Mexico.

CONCLUSION

To be successful, NAFTA will require a strong trilateral trade mechanism, independent of national influences, for resolving disputes. The long-term national-security interests of the United States are best served by neighbors who enjoy the social stability that a successful NAFTA, by stimulating growth among its members, would accomplish. A growing and stable Mexican economy is also the best, and perhaps the only, way to manage South–North migration. A dynamic Mexican economy would continue to turn to the United States for its imports. Finally, the North American market created by NAFTA has the potential to meet—even to beat—the best products other trading nations have to offer. Even such old-line industries as textiles and footwear could find new fame and fortune by strategically placing production throughout the United States, Canada, and Mexico.

Worry about passage of NAFTA is not confined to the United States, Canada, and Mexico but runs all the way to South America. In 1990, when President Bush proposed making NAFTA into a hemisphere-wide free trade zone, Latin American governments welcomed the suggestion. They reduced trade barriers and introduced internal economic reforms in hope of speeding their admission to the free trade club.

If so much could be said in favor of NAFTA, why so much opposition to it? The answer to this perplexing question is deeply hidden in human behavior, narrow self-interest, fear, and sometimes ignorance to see the entire picture, as well as failure to take a long-term view. While groups who gain from protection can persuade policymakers that their private interests coincide with the national interest, the protectionist attitude will continue to stultify the flow of trade among nations who are otherwise committed to competitive market economies. Similarly, the struggle for freer trade is a never-ending chronology of victories and defeats with no outcome.

We are in transition, adjusting from the Cold War era to new global cooperation. The old ways of thinking about the world no longer work. Nowadays we must think globally, trade globally, and compete globally. NAFTA is the most extensive, visionary response to this new economic reality.

Though the agreement does make much business sense, there is a strong emotional opposition to it by many Americans. The anti-NAFTA movement is spearheaded by Ross Perot, who argues that the United States will lose much-needed jobs to Mexico because of it. According to Perot, even though NAFTA has been ratified by the Senate, this will only be temporary; eventually, the agreement should be rescinded because of massive public opposition (Perot 1992). Some of Perot's own family members do not agree with his viewpoints on NAFTA (Moffett and Obdyke 1993).

APPENDIX C

Pioneers in Quality

Product quality is essential to Total Quality Marketing, and the latter cannot function without the former. Therefore, this section reviews the background and philosophies of some pioneers in quality control management. In addition, it discusses certain important developments such as the more recent Japanese contribution to quality.

Crosby

Philip Crosby defines quality as "conformance to requirements." In service companies, for example, "the waste goes out in baskets, and in manufacturing it goes out in barrels" (Crosby 1979, p. 15).

Deming

W. Edward Deming is a consultant and a Distinguished Professor of Management at Columbia University. Born on October 14, 1900, in Sioux City, Iowa, he received a Ph.D. in mathematical physics from Yale University in 1928. He also received the Order of Sacred Treasure, 2nd Class (Japan) in 1960.

During the 1950s, Edward Deming made several trips to Japan to instruct the Japanese on controlling quality in production. His important message was that quality problems can be controlled through a rigorous and systematic statistical process control. Going beyond statistical instruction, he encouraged firms to use a systematic approach to problem solving. This is known as "Plan, Do, Check, Action (PDCA) or Deming Cycle" (Deming 1982, pp. 101–104). He pushed top managers to get involved in a firm's quality programs and introduced modern methods of consumer research.

Juran

Joseph M. Juran is Chairperson Emeritus, Juran Institute, Inc. He was born on December 24, 1904, in Braila, Romania, and holds a B.S. degree in electrical engineering from the University of Minnesota and a J.D. degree from Loyola University at Chicago. He was also a recipient of the Order of Sacred Treasure, 2nd Class (Japan) in 1981.

Like Deming, Juran was invited to lecture in Japan during the 1950s. His lectures focused on planning, organizational issues, management's responsibility for quality, and the need to set goals and targets for general quality improvement on a project basis. Thus Juran imbued in the minds of the Japanese "the basic philosophy of planning quality" (1974).

According to Juran, we have a quality crisis. The guru of international quality movement explains what keeps going wrong with so many American efforts at Total Quality Management. Only a few of America's major companies have attained world-class quality—less than 50 of the Fortune 500. And even fewer of the general population of corporations have attained this goal. The remaining companies are in various stages of their quality journeys. Some have not yet started. Some are starting over. Some have begun to make progress. Some are well along. Others have tried, failed, and given up (1993, pp. 35–38).

The most dramatic evidence of the quality crisis in the Western world has been the superior quality of many Japanese products. Because of their quality revolution, the Japanese manufacturers could outperform their Western competitors. Japan offered higher-quality goods to the same customers for whom Western companies were competing at equal or lower prices. That revolution did much damage to U.S. companies. It reduced their market shares, contributed to a severe decline in the balance of trade, and resulted in the export of many U.S. jobs overseas.

There are other contributors to the quality crisis. One is the growth of international competition, generally fueled by the rise of multinational companies. A more subtle contributor has been the growth of industrialized societies. Such societies redesign their lifestyles to secure the benefits of technological products. In turn, these societies require failure-free performance to maintain continuity of services, to protect against disruption in their lives, and to avoid disaster.

Why have the companies that tried to enact quality programs so often failed? If we are going to fight a war, after all, it is a good idea to know who the enemy is.

Many CEOs of the 1980s realized that the quality crisis called for a solid response—a counterrevolution in quality. However, most of those CEOs lacked knowledge of what to do and were ignorant in the best sense of that word. This ignorance is readily explained.

About a century ago, the Taylor system of management that separates planning from execution emerged in the United States. Although it helped the United States to become the world leader in productivity, the Taylor system was also damaging to quality as it is known today. In response, our companies created the central inspection department that then evolved into the quality department of today. It then became convenient to delegate the responsibility for quality to those quality departments. As a by-product, the CEOs became detached from the problems of managing for quality. They were out of the loop and remained so for decades, a situation that produced ignorance of how to manage for quality.

As the quality crisis grew, it took a growing toll of market share. The record of the past shows that preoccupation with protectionism seldom improves competitiveness and that sometimes it even damages public relations. During the

1992 visit of President Bush to Japan, some CEOs of leading U.S. companies who went along with him on the trip complained that the Japanese market was closed to them, and they had evidence to support that complaint. Yet, the media focused on the spectacle of the CEOs of our automobile companies complaining at a time when they lacked right-hand-drive cars to sell in Japan.

Unsuccessful companies did not consider quality or customer satisfaction as top priorities. Although recognizing that quality is very important, unsuccessful companies did not include quality-related goals. They did not include goals such as improving customer satisfaction, meeting competitive quality, reducing the cost of poor quality, or improving major processes. Nor did they integrate managing for quality.

Unsuccessful companies did not use benchmarks to set ambitious quality goals. In addition, many goals were ludicrously unattainable. These companies focused exclusively on financial measures—sales, profits, return on investment—and they lacked some essential measures of quality. These are measures of customer satisfaction and competitive quality. Lacking these, they learned of their quality problems only after severe damage had already occurred. Also, these firms did not establish a regular executive review of performance against the quality goals, paralleling the review of performance against the financial goals.

Indeed, unsuccessful companies did not conduct self-audits. They did not identify the strengths and weaknesses of their divisions and their support services. Thus, none of this information was available to be input into decision making. Companies that did attempt such self-audits failed to measure themselves against strict and uniform criteria.

Many companies did not give public acknowledgment to persons and teams who achieved superior performance. Nor did they revise the reward system to reflect the job changes inherent in the quality initiative. They neglect to train subordinate managers while managing for quality. Those that did train did not train their entire managerial hierarchy to manage for quality, quality planning, quality control, and quality improvement. Lacking such training and experience, they were seriously hindered; and the quality goals remained a wish list.

Many companies also refused to use self-directed teams. They may have trained empowered workers, but those same workers were not allowed to run processes. With less supervision than before (substantially demotivating otherwise good workers), unsuccessful organizations also resisted partnerships with suppliers. They missed the revolution in supplier relations and remained adversaries. They were not willing to share information or participate in joint planning and improvement projects. Unsuccessful companies did not look thoroughly at business-process quality management. During the 1980s, there emerged a new finding. Many quality problems are more traceable to business processes than to factory processes. Unsuccessful companies refused to shrink their supplier base to include only those suppliers who took quality improvement seriously. Many companies did not even have the courage to serve notice to the colleges that supply them with the bulk of their recruits.

The CEOs of unsuccessful companies did not personally participate in setting quality goals, nor did they approve the final goals. Also, they neither participated in the deployment process nor approved the resulting action plans. They did not approve allocation of the needed resources. They did not assign responsibility for establishing either the new measure needed to quantify the quality goal or the measure needed to judge performance against those goals. They did not participate in revising the reward system to make it responsive to the changes imposed by the quality initiative. The large corporations failed to assess the relations between the corporations and the autonomous divisions.

Successful CEOs increasingly use the following managerial sequence. First, establish the vision and policies; next, train the hierarchy; next, establish the goals to be met; then, plan how to reach the goals and provide the resources. The final step in the sequence should be to manage and measure quality as seriously as one would profitability.

Deming–Juran Rivalry

For more than four decades, Deming and Juran have been the preeminent champions of quality. While they cross paths often and maintain an air of cordiality, beneath the surface they are keen rivals.

Deming, the senior guru of statistical quality control (SQC), towers over Juran in both physical stature and fame. He is, after all, the namesake of Japan's Deming prize. It was created in 1951, just after his first lecture tour there, and quickly became Japan's most coveted industrial award. A spry workaholic in his nineties, Deming has a legendary caustic temper that flares at the suggestion that Juran's ideas have much merit or staying power.

Along with his trademark BMW tie, Juran is best known for being the elder diplomat of total quality control (TQC). He too has found his most loyal following in Japan, where he first described his method in 1954. While Deming's three-year lead there has won him more notice, many people feel that Juran's influence has been greater over the years. In 1969, acknowledging Juran's role, a super prize, the Juran Medal, was created to match the Deming Prize.

Despite their differences, Deming and Juran have lived parallel lives. Both came from humble origins: Deming grew up in a tarpaper-covered shack near Cody, Wyoming; Juran in a tarpaper shack near Minneapolis. Both got into the quality game by chance. In the mid-1920s, both men took jobs with Western Electric Company. Both came under the influence of Walter A. Shewhat, the AT&T Bell Laboratories physicist who was turning statistical concepts that originated in agricultural research into a manufacturing discipline. After World War II, both Deming and Juran became independent consultants.

Deming still runs a one-man show from a Washington, D.C., office surrounded by his disciples. In 1986, he began videotaping selected lectures and conversations with other quality experts. These have been made available from Films Inc. in Chicago. He still attends Deming prize ceremonies each October in Tokyo.

Juran ended his one-man act in 1979 and founded the Juran Institute Inc. to carry on his life's work and build a library of videotapes and training materials. In 1989, he stepped down from the Wilton, Connecticut, Institute. He passed the baton—actually, one of his BMW ties—to A. Blanton Godfrey, former head of quality theory at Bell Labs. Since then, Juran has worked mainly at home on history of management and on his memoirs of the quality revolution.

For Japan, merely reliable goods are no longer good enough. From hand-painted vases to high-tech design and assembly of bike frames, attention to detail is the hallmark of Japanese quality. Japanese auto companies, for example, have been moving aggressively from quality that is taken for granted to quality that fascinates.

In 40 years, a focus on quality has turned Japan from a maker of knickknacks into an economic powerhouse—and U.S. and European companies are being forced to respond. The result has been a global revolution affecting every facet of business. Clearly, high quality lowers total costs while improving the products and services. For the 1990s and far beyond, quality must remain the priority for business (*Business Week* 1991, p. 7).

At a recent conference in Tokyo, Juran made a rare prediction. Surveying an audience mostly of Japanese executives who have used his quality control methods to humble their U.S. competitors, he declared that America is about to bounce back. In the 1990s, he said, "Made in the U.S.A" will become a symbol of world-class quality again. Even if the United States does not catch up with Japan, he expects big gains in competitiveness. "When 30% of U.S. products were failures vs. 3% for Japan, it is an enormous difference. But at failures of 0.3% and .03%, it'd be difficult for any one to tell" (*Business Week* 1991, p. 8).

It remains to be seen if Juran's vision will be fulfilled. Major industries in the United States and Europe are trying to prove him right. These awakened giants see an urgent need to match the close-to-perfection standard set by Japan after 40 years of dogged effort. Catching up with Japan may be almost incidental to the mere effort of trying that will in many ways change the way business is done.

Already, business schools are revamping their MBA programs to reflect their new thrust. One after another, U.S. companies are establishing an office called vice president for quality. Gross deficiencies turned up by the four-year-old Baldrige quality award competition, a response to Japan's 40-year-old Deming prize, are being taken to heart. There is now widespread realization that quality simply isn't implicit in the way U.S. companies design and make products or the way they treat customers.

An ironic sign of quality push is that the focus on quality is going beyond the "us vs. them" mentality. Here and there, a new philosophy is taking hold—excellence should be the norm, not the exception. Motorola, Inc., for example, may soon adopt an unheard of goal—60 defects for every billion components it makes.

Quality is not hard to define: it is simply the absence of variation. Thus, a Chevrolet can have just as much quality as a Rolls-Royce, and the service at a discount store can be as "good"—free of variations—as that at Bergdorf-Goodman.

Trade barriers that include tariff and nontariff barriers include (1) tariffs; (2) quotas; (3) voluntary restraints; (4) boycotts; (5) monetary barriers (differential exchange rates, approval requirements for foreign exchange for imports); and (6) standards in health, safety, and product qualities, which are often used to restrict imports entering the country.

O'Neil, of ALCOA, argues that as trade barriers come down worldwide competition will intensify. Only companies with the finest quality will thrive—and not because of quality alone (*Business Week* 1991, pp. 8–9). Two by-products of making or doing things better are usually lower costs and higher productivity.

Until recently, many such efforts were delayed by the mistaken belief that better quality costs more. Since excellence is measured by lack of defects, in an inspection-oriented plant, more than half of all workers are somehow involved in finding and reworking rejects. The total investment in this process can account for 20 percent to 35 percent of production costs—in extreme cases to 50 percent.

The Japanese, following the advice of Deming and Juran, devised a cheaper system. They inspect a product before it is made—in the design stage—and they engineer the manufacturing process to be stable and reliable. If the design is good and so is the process, quality is inherent.

In the United States, SQC was used widely during World War II. After the war, companies were too busy to bother. Swamped by pent-up demand, they cranked out products and let quality fend for itself.

The Japanese, meanwhile, were getting ahead. They bought into Juran's idea of total quality control—applying quality principles not just in the factory but to every operation, including dealings with suppliers. Consequently, Toyota Motor Co. vice president Taichi Ohno and industrial consultant Shiego Shingo devised Toyota's Kanban system, which blossomed into the just-in-time movement. The idea behind JIT is delivering parts to an assembly line at just the moment they're needed. This holds down costs, but it requires consistently high quality throughout the supply chain (*Business Week* 1991, pp. 8–9).

Feigenbaum

Armand Feigenbaum, then head of quality control at GE, argued for a systematic and total approach to quality. He wanted the involvement of all functions in the quality process. Otherwise, Feigenbaum claimed, quality would be inspected and controlled after the fact and not built in at an early stage (1983).

These three American leaders have significantly contributed to the highly successful Japanese quality movement. Together, Juran and Feigenbaum awakened the Japanese to the less statistical aspects of quality management.

THE JAPANESE CONTRIBUTION TO
QUALITY REVOLUTION

The Japanese ultimately developed a quality movement that was uniquely their own (Garvin 1988, pp. 182–184). In fact, several recent innovations such as quality (Q) control circles came in the late 1950s and early 1960s and were invented by the Japanese.

They successfully carried out these ideas because they had strong support from various government organizations, such as the Union of Japanese Scientists and Engineers, the Ministry for International Trade and Industry (MITI), and the powerful business associations. One important Japanese innovation in their relentless pursuit of quality was the Q circle.

Quality Circles

A Q circle is a small group of employees doing similar work under one supervisor who meet regularly to identify, analyze, and solve product quality problems (Rieker 1977). They are participatory problem-solving groups. The circles follow the theory that people take more interest in and place higher value on their work if they are allowed to make decisions about it. Furthermore, this theory assumes that those who work on a particular job know best how to make improvements (Harnac and Brannen 1982, pp. 67–68).

Theoretically, Q circles are voluntary. Each circle consists of about ten people who meet weekly. Training for both leaders and members involves learning various techniques of giving management presentations. In addition, the training includes brainstorms, cause-and-effect diagrams, Pareto diagrams, histograms, check sheets, graphs, sampling, and control charts to analyze the sources and cause of quality problems.

Introduced into the United States in the mid-1980s, Q circles have not been as effective as they are in Japan because of social and cultural differences (Callahan 1982, p. 107). In the United States, workers are individualistic and self-centered, whereas the Japanese are group-centered and self-sacrificing. Thus, Q circles work better in the Japanese and similar social environments.

A concept like that of the quality circle is easy to understand. To operationalize such a concept, however, each country must individually develop a system that corresponds to its distinctive social and cultural environment. It must be recognized that certain subjective factors, such as unique social and cultural characteristics, can often influence a country's economic competitiveness and achievement. For example, in Japan, the interaction of three major behavioral variables—Japanese attitudes toward work, achievement, and adaptability—enabled them to achieve the "economic miracle" (Reddy, Rao, Oliver, and Addington 1984, p. 45). The Japanese model is now being emulated by other East Asian countries with similar social and cultural characteristics with impressive success.

Poka-Yoke

Japanese quality expert Shingo introduced an idea called poka-yoke, a way to minimize human error. For instance, if a car's headlights were designed to make them look awkward when installed, poka-yoke would call for a change in the design. United Electric Controls Co., a maker of industrial sensors and controls in Watertown, Massachusetts, and a recent Shingo convert, has added beveled edges to parts so that they can be assembled only the correct way, helping slash delivery time from twelve weeks to three days. These ideas, though they relate to production quality directly, have application to marketing quality as well in terms of the approach and discipline needed to maintain a consistent quality.

A more radical approach comes from Genichi Taguchi, a well-known Japanese engineering consultant. He calls it "robust design." Taguchi argues (Taguchi and Clausing 1990) that missing the quality target consistently is better than hitting it, at least when allowable deviations are scattered throughout the area. He uses the analogy of two sharpshooters: one always hits a 6-inch-diameter bull's eye, but the shots are scattered from edge to edge. The other hits the bull's eye less often, but all shots are grouped in a 3-inch circle. The latter would win without competition if he adjusts his rifle's sights.

Consistency is critical, Taguchi insists, because of a rule of thumb called the quality loss function which holds that any deviation from dead center, no matter how small, increases a product's ultimate costs, including warranty liability and lost customer goodwill. Although Taguchi's insights have been a staple of Japanese engineering education for three decades, they were almost unknown in the United States until 1983 when Ford Motor Co. began teaching them to its engineers. Only now are they catching on broadly. That is why many U.S. and European manufacturers find themselves sitting where the Japanese were a decade or two ago (*Business Week* 1991, pp. 10–11).

According to Juran (1993), the Japanese did not learn about quality from him or from Edward Deming, as is generally believed to be true in the West. Juran believes that the idea of quality was already there in the Japanese culture and that all he and Deming did was to reinforce it. In the context, Japanese had three types of quality: one for war machines, one for the consumer goods industry, and one for consumer goods. In World War II, their Zero aircraft and ammunition were of very high quality though their consumer products were shoddy and factory floors were not up to level. After the war, they invested heavily in modernizing their consumer-goods-producing factories and improved consumer-goods product quality to near perfection.

Shanklin (1989, p. 28) feels that improving product quality alone does not guarantee success and prosperity. Shanklin further believes that Frank Perdue built his family's small chicken-producing operation into the fifth-largest company in its industry by observing quality in total marketing effort. Growth is achieved by combining a zeal for product quality with aggressive and innovative marketing and by making right decisions and implementing them right every time.

Maytag is another company that has clearly proved that quality sells in the marketplace. These days, however, consumers expect not only high quality in a given product or service but also low price and other quality-driven marketing mix strategies. In today's global competition with intense media scrutiny, no company can compete by selling shoddy products. Today's more educated and demanding consumers want to know "where's the beef?" the question asked in the classic Wendy's hamburger advertisement.

Firms cannot get by selling the sizzle alone without having a good quality product. A marketer like Michelin sells both steak and sizzle instead of the steak or sizzle. Strong psychological appeals to people's needs and wants, accompanied by intrinsic product quality, are necessary for marketing effectiveness. Steak without some sizzle will usually not attract customers even in business-to-business marketing. But sizzle without steak is a sure recipe for failure.

Emphasizing the sizzle at the expense of quality has put several American firms into deep trouble, especially with foreign competition. It took the auto industry almost three decades first to retain its market shares and then to begin regaining the lost shares. While the Japanese automakers sold their cars on quality, value, and economy during the 1970s and 1980s, the U.S. automakers were using exotic promotions by using movie celebrities like Farrah Fawcett to sell their cars.

All segments of consumers are alike in one important way despite their varying lifestyles. Whether one is a doctor, lawyer, production-line employee, or whatever, consumers want one thing—products that work and services that serve.

A company can build a whole corporate strategy around quality. The issue of quality can be a common goal and a bond among all corporate functions—from production to sales and everything that supports them. Consequently, quality needs to be the daily concern of all employees, from the CEO to the newest hire in maintenance. This achievement is easier said than done, of course, and requires careful employee selection, continual employee training, and a facilitating corporate culture. Union–management relations in one prominent airline became so strained at one point that some employees decided to get even with management by doing a poor job. No amount of training could rectify this kind of distrust (Shanklin 1989, pp. 37–38).

One should never advertise product quality if it is not there. Puffery and exaggeration are sure to come back to haunt the company that makes claims its products and services cannot justify. From a marketing standpoint, there is nothing worse than unconfirmed customer expectations (Shanklin 1989, p. 38). Japanese companies that assemble automobiles in the United States (Honda, Nissan, and others) outperform Ford in quality surveys of car owners. Ford says it has "designed and built" the best-quality cars and trucks in the United States—which is technically true: The Japanese cars are built in the United States but designed in Japan (Shanklin 1989, p. 39).

TQM is the only source of enduring competitive advantage in today's world. Pankaj Ghemwat (1986) categorizes these advantages into three groups: (1) size in the targeted market, (2) better access to resources and customers, and (3) restrictions on competitor options.

To exploit commitment opportunities, a business can preempt its competitors. The business, however, must be especially wary of environmental changes that can erode the value of its early investments. Size can be an advantage only when there are compelling advantages to being large such as economies of scale, scope, or experience. Advantages through preferred access to resources, information, or customers can give a business a sustainable advantage independent of size. Furthermore, restriction on options available to competitors might occasionally arise, limiting their ability to imitate the lead company's strategy. Rivals can be frozen into their current position for several reasons—by restrictive public policies, by their inability to defend their positions, and by the response lags.

A survey in 1981 found that nearly 50 percent of American consumers felt that the quality of U.S. products dropped during the previous five years (Binstock 1981, p. 13). Another survey, made by Gallup in 1985, found that consumers would pay about one-third more for a better quality car; 50 percent more for a better quality dishwasher; proportionately more for a television set or sofa; and twice the list price for better-quality shoes. The study also found that people with higher incomes were far more dissatisfied with the quality of American products (Peters 1987, p. 83).

"Quality" is thus fast becoming a primary competitive issue of the 1990s (Garvin 1988). The label "Made in U.S.A." once represented an assurance of quality and reliability. Unfortunately, for many people in recent years, it has become a warning. As incidents of shoddy workmanship and defective products in U.S. goods keep increasing, dissatisfied consumers and industrial buyers turn to imports as alternatives. It is a pattern that cuts across all income and educational levels, ideologies, and national pride. Wealthy Americans want the German Mercedes and the budget-conscious prefer a Korean Hyundai. People who are most avid proponents of "buy America" buy Japanese appliances, Italian shoes, and Taiwanese sports clothes without hesitation.

The drive for higher quality is a result of several new factors: modern consumers are better educated, smarter, more discriminating, and more demanding and no longer susceptible to intimidation by the store or the supplier. In addition, advances in technology make product quality and reliability normal, expected conditions (Kami 1988, p. 105). Professor E. Cole made this scathing remark in comparing American-made automobiles with European and Japanese makes. "The best of ours [now] are about as good as the worst of theirs, and that is a tremendous achievement" (Peters 1987, p. 79); for example, Mitsubishi's Precis compared with Chevrolet's Corsica—"the heartbeat of America."

Such quality problems are pervasive in most American firms and are not limited to a single industry. In his book, *Thriving on Chaos*, Tom Peters points out: "For the most part, the quality of made-in-America goods and services is questionable; perhaps 'stinks' is often a more accurate word. Yet, fifteen years after the battering began, quality is still not often truly at the top of the American corporate agenda" (1987, p. 81).

Some experts warn that unless American firms match or better quality levels achieved by foreign competitors, the U.S. industry and the economy are bound to suffer. Yet many American firms disregard this important message and ignore quality. According to a survey of several hundred large institutional investors, earnings ranked first and quality last among factors that influence stock selection (Factor 1985, p. 28). Such investor biases further influence U.S. manufactures to neglect quality.

From the viewpoint of customers, getting a defective product and having to complain about it is a nuisance. Customers simply refuse to suffer such inconvenience of waiting for someone to fix the problem. They buy alternative brands with better quality and reputation. The Japanese experience clearly showed that it is less costly to make the product right in the first place than to fix it after a customer has bought it. Quality does not mean meeting assembly-line inspection standards during manufacturing. Products must be designed to meet customer needs from the start. One defective automobile part in 10,000 may not seem like much; but if that part keeps a completed car from starting at the end of the production line, finding the problem can be very costly.

Firms that adopted TQM methods to reduce manufacturing defects soon used the same approaches to overcome many other implementation problems. Their success brought attention to what is possible with TQM—whether the implementation problem concerns unreliable delivery schedules, poor customer service, advertising that appears on the wrong TV show, or salespeople who cannot answer customers' questions. The idea of doing things right the first time seems obvious, but it is easier said than done.

CONCLUSION

Quality, whether it is in marketing or management, is multidimensional. One must view it from many sides before plunging into action to make quality improvements.

References

American Society for Quality Control (1988). *Gallup Survey: Consumers' Perceptions Concerning the Quality of American Products and Services*. Milwaukee: American Society for Quality Control.

Ansoff, H. Igor (1988). *The New Corporate Strategy*. New York: John Wiley.

Assael, Henry (1987). *Consumer Behavior and Marketing Action*, third edition. Boston: PWS-Kent.

Batra, Ravi (1993). *The Myth of Free Trade: A Plan for America's Economic Revival*. New York: Charles Scribner's Sons/Macmillan.

Bell, D. E., R. L. Keeney, and J. D. C. Little (1975). "A Market Share Theorem." *Journal of Marketing Research* 12 (May): 136–141.

Bergsten, C., and William R. Cline (1987). *The United States–Japan Economic Problems*. Washington, D.C.: Institution for International Economics.

Berkowitz, Eric, Roger A. Kerin, Steven W. Hartley, and William Rudelius (1992). *Marketing*, 3rd ed. Homewood, Ill.: Richard D. Irwin.

Berry, Leonard (1986). "Big Ideas in Services Marketing." *Journal of Consumer Marketing* 3 (Spring): 47–51.

Berry, Leonard, Jeffrey S. Conant, and A. Parasuraman (1991). "Framework for Conducting a Service Marketing Audit." *Journal of the Academy of Marketing Science* 19 (Summer): 255–269.

Berry, Leonard, and A. Parasuraman (1992). "Prescriptions for a Service Quality Revolution in America." *Organizational Dynamics* 20 (Spring): 5–16.

Binstock, S. L. (1981). "American's Express Dissatisfaction with Quality of U.S. Goods." *Quality Progress*, January, p. 13.

Bitner, Mary Jo (1992). "The Impact of Physical Surroundings on Customers and Employers." *Journal of Marketing* 56 (April): 57–72.

Bitner, Mary Jo, Bernard H. Booms, and Mary S. Tetreault (1990). "The Service Encounter: Diagnosing Favorable and Unfavorable Incidents." *Journal of Marketing* 54 (January): 71–85.

Buier, Martin, Pet Hoke, and Bob Stone (1993). "Direct Marketing—What Is It?" *Direct Marketing* (January): 5.

Burton, Daniel F., Jr. (1989). "Economic Realities and Strategic Choices." In Burton, Daniel F., Jr., Victor Gotbaum, and Felix G. Rhatyn, eds., *Vision for the 1990s: U.S. Strategy and the Global Economy*. Cambridge, Mass.: Ballinger, pp. 3–25.

Business Week (1987). "An Electronic Pipeline That Is Changing the Way America Does Business." August 1, p. 80.

———. (1991). "The Quality Imperative." October 25, pp. 58–61.

Buzzell, Robert D., and Frederick D. Wiersema (1981). "Successful Share Building." *Harvard Business Review* 59 (January-February): 135–144.

Bylinsky, Gene (1989). "Where Japan Will Strike Next." *Fortune* (September): 25.

Callahan, Robert E. (1982). "Quality Circles: A Program for Productivity through Human Resources Development." In Lee, Sang M., and Gary Schwendiman, eds., *Management by Japanese Systems*. New York: Praeger.

Cateora, Philip (1993). *International Marketing*, 8th ed. Homewood, Ill.: Richard D. Irwin.

Cohen, Stephen D. (1985). *Uneasy Partnership: Competition and Conflict in U.S. Japanese Trade Relations*. Cambridge, Mass.: Ballinger.

Corning, Peter, and Susan Corning (1986). *Winning with Synergy: How America Can Regain the Competitive Edge*. San Francisco: Harper & Row.

Cravens, David W. (1994). *Strategic Marketing*, 4th ed. Burr Ridge, Ill.: Richard Irwin, Inc.

Crosby, Philip B. (1979). *Quality Is Free*. New York: McGraw-Hill.

Cunningham, William (1986). "Some Potential Problems in Just-in-Time Inventory Systems: An Initial Investigation." *Business Insights* (Fall): 20–21.

Daft, Richard L. (1991). *Management*, 2nd ed. Chicago, Ill.: The Dryden Press.

Deming, Edward (1982). *Quality, Productivity, and Competitive Position*. Cambridge: MIT Press.

Dodds, William B., and Kent B. Monroe (1985). "The Effect of Brand and Price Information on Subjective Product Evaluations." In Advances in Consumer Research, vol. 12. Provo, Utah: Association for Consumer Research, pp. 85–90.

Duro, Robert, and Bjorn Sandstrom (1987). *The Basic Principles of Marketing Warfare*. New York: John Wiley.

The Economist (1987). "The Export of Japanese Ideas." (April): 34–35, 68.

Evans, Joel R., and Barry Berman (1992). *Marketing*, 5th ed. New York: Macmillan.

Factor, Mallory (1985). "Wall Street Must Choose between Quality and the Fast Buck." *Wall Street Journal*, April 15, p. 18.

Feigenbaum, A. V. (1983). *Total Quality Control*, 3rd ed. New York: McGraw-Hill.

Frazier, Gary L., Robert E. Spekman, and Charles R. O'Neal (1988). "Just-in-Time Exchange Relationships in Industrial Markets." *Journal of Marketing* (October): 52–67.

Gale, Robert D., and Robert D. Buzzell (1989). "Market Perceived Quality: Key Strategic Concept." *Planning Review* 17 (March-April): 6–15, 48.

Garvin, David A. (1988). *Managing Quality: The Strategic and Competitive Edge*. New York: Free Press.

Ghemwat, Pankaj (1986). "Sustainable Advantage." *Harvard Business Review* 86 (September-October): 53–58.

Glickman, Norman J., and Douglas P. Woodward (1989). *The New Competitors: How Foreign Investors Are Changing the U.S. Economy.* New York: Basic Books.

Godfrey, Blanton A., and Peter J. Kolesar (1988). "Role of Quality in Achieving World Class Competitiveness." In Starr, Martin K., ed., *Global Competitiveness: Getting the U.S. Back on Track.* New York: W. W. Norton, pp. 213–238.

Hall, Edward T., and Mildred Reed Hall (1990). *Hidden Differences: Doing Business with the Japanese.* New York: Anchor Press/Doubleday.

Harnac, Jo Ann, and Kathleen C. Brannen (1982). "The What, Where, and Whys of Quality Control Circles." In Lee, Sang M., and Gary Schwendiman, eds., *Management by Japanese Systems.* New York: Praeger, pp. 67–75.

Harrington, H. J. (1987). *The Improvement Process: How America's Leading Companies Improve Quality.* New York: McGraw-Hill.

Hayes, Robert H., Kim B. Clark, and Christopher Lorens, eds. (1985). *The Uneasy Alliance: Managing the Productivity-Technology Dilemma.* Boston: Harvard Business School Press.

Hichings, Robert H. (1987). "The Application of an Effective Inquiry Handling System for Business-to-Business Marketing." *Journal of Direct Marketing* 1 (Spring): 51–59.

Holbrook, Morris B., and Kim P. Korfman (1985). "Quality and Value in the Consumption Experience: Phraedus Rides Again." In Jacoby, Jacob, and Jerry Olson, eds., *Perceived Quality: How Consumers View Stores and Merchandise.* Lexington, Mass.: Lexington Books, pp. 31–57.

Inman, Anthony (1991). "Just-in-Time: Alive and Well in the South." *The Southern Business and Economic Journal* (April): 155–165.

Juran, Joseph M. (1993). "Why Quality Initiatives Fail." *Journal of Business Strategy* 14 (July-August): 35–38.

——, ed. (1974). *Quality Control Handbook,* 3rd ed. New York: McGraw-Hill.

Kami, Michael J. (1988). *Trigger Points: How to Make Decisions Three Times Faster, Innovate Smarter, and Beat Your Competition by Ten Percent (It Ain't Easy!).* New York: McGraw-Hill.

Kano, Noriaki (1993). "Quality as Value Added to Sales Rather Than Saving Cost Reduction." *Quality Management Journal* 1 (October): 56–62.

Karmarkar, Uday (1989). "Getting Control of Just-in-Time." *Harvard Business Review* 67 (September-October): 122–132.

Kotler, Philip (1988). *Marketing Management: Analysis, Planning, Implementation, and Control,* 6th ed. Englewood Cliffs, N.J.: Prentice-Hall.

——. (1991). *Marketing Management: Analysis, Planning, Implementation, and Control,* 7th ed. Englewood Cliffs, N.J.: Prentice-Hall.

Kotler, Philip, and Ravi Sing (1981). "Marketing Warfare." *Journal of Business Strategy* 1 (Winter): 30–41.

Kotler, Philip, Liam Fahey, and S. Jatusripitak (1985). *The New Competition.* Englewood Cliffs, N.J.: Prentice-Hall.

Krishna, E. M., and C. P. Rao (1986). "Is U.S. High Technology High Enough?" *Columbia Journal of World Business* 21 (Summer): 47–54.

Lambert, Zarrell V. (1970). "Product Perception: An Important Variable in Pricing Strategy." *Journal of Marketing* 34 (October): 68–71.

Larson, Paul D. (1989). "Quality Improvement: The Role of Marketing." Paper presented at the AMA Summer Marketing Educators' Conference, Chicago, Ill., August 6–9.

Levitt, Arthur, Jr., and Gordon C. Stewart (1988). "Can American Business Compete? A Perspective of Mid-Range Growth Companies." In Starr, Martin K., ed., *Global Competitiveness: Getting the U.S. Back on Track*. New York: W. W. Norton, pp. 271–278.

Levitt, Theodore (1981). "Making Intangible Products and Product Intangibles." *Harvard Business Review* 67 (May-June): 94–102.

Lovelock, Christopher H. (1991). *Services Marketing*. Englewood Cliffs, N.J.: Prentice-Hall.

Magaziner, Ira C. (1989). *The Silent War: Inside the Global Business Battles Shaping America's Future*. New York: Random House.

Marketing News (1986). "Wal-Mart Credits Deep Discounts to Hub-and-Spoke Planning." June 20, p. 10.

McCarthy, E. Jerome, and William D. Perrault, Jr. (1993). *Basic Marketing: A Global-Managerial Approach*. Homewood, Ill.: Richard D. Irwin.

McConnell, Campbell R., and Stanley L. Brue (1990). *Economics: Principles, Problems, and Policies*, 11th ed. New York: McGraw-Hill.

McConnell, Douglas J. (1968). "Effect of Pricing on Perception of Product Quality." *Journal of Applied Psychology* 52 (August): 331–334.

McCullough, Rachel (1985). "Trade Deficits, Industrial Competitiveness, and the Japanese." *California Management Review* 27 (Winter): 140–156.

McGrath, Allan J. (1988). *Market Smarts: Proven Strategies to Outfox and Outflank Your Competition*. New York: John Wiley.

Michaelson, Gerald A. (1987). *Winning the Marketing War: A Field Manual for Business Leaders*. Lanham, Md.: Abt Books.

Moffett, Matt, and Jeff D. Obdyke (1993). "Perot's Stand against Trade Shared by Pact with Mexico Isn't Shared by Business Owned by His Family." *Wall Street Journal*, July 6, p. A8.

Monroe, Kent B. (1976). "The Influence of Price Differences and Brand Familiarity on Brand Preferences." *Journal of Consumer Research* 3 (June): 42–49.

Monroe, Kent B., and R. Krishnan (1985). "The Effect of Price on Subjective Product Evaluations." In Jacoby, Jacob, and Jerry Olson, eds., *Perceived Quality: How Consumers View Stores and Merchandise*. Lexington, Mass.: Lexington Books, pp. 209–232.

Monroe, Kent B., and Williams B. Dodds (1988). "A Research Program for Establishing the Price-Quality Relationship." *Journal of the Academy of Marketing Sciences* 19 (Spring): 151–168.

Nimgade, Ashok (1989). "American Management as Viewed by International Professionals." *Business Horizons* 32 (November-December): 98–105.

O'Grady, Peter J. (1988). *Putting the Just-in-Time Philosophy into Practice*. New York: Nicholls Publishing Company.

Parasuraman, A., Valerie A. Zeithaml, and Leonard L. Berry (1986). "SERVQUAL: A Multiple-Item Scale for Measuring Customer Perceptions of Service Quality." Marketing Science Institute Report No. 86, Cambridge, Mass.

Parasuraman, A., Valerie A. Zeithaml, and Leonard L. Berry (1991). "Understanding Customer Expectations of Service." *Sloan Management Review* 32 (Spring): 39–49.

Partner, Simon (1992). *Saying Yes to Japanese Management.* Englewood Cliffs, N.J.: Prentice-Hall.

Perot, Ross (1992). *Not for Sale at Any Price.* New York: Hyperion.

Peters, Tom (1987). *Thriving on Chaos.* New York: Harper & Row.

Pitts, Robert A., and Charles C. Snow (1986). *Strategies for Competitive Success.* New York: John Wiley & Sons.

Porter, Michael E. (1990). "The Competitive Advantage of Nations." *Harvard Business Review* 68 (March-April): 73–93.

Prahalad, C. K., and Gary Hamel (1990). "The Core Competence of the Corporation." *Harvard Business Review* 68 (May-June): 79–91.

Pride, William M., and O. C. Ferrell (1991). *Marketing Concepts and Strategies,* 7th ed. Boston: Houghton Mifflin.

Ram, S., and Jagdish N. Sheth (1989). "Consumer Resistance to Innovations: The Marketing Problem and Its Solutions." *Journal of Consumer Marketing* 6 (Spring): 5–14.

Reddy, Allan C., C. P. Rao, and Niren P. Vyas (1992). "Just-in-Time (JIT) Retailing." In Crittenden, Victoria L., ed., *Developments in Marketing Science,* vol. 15. San Diego: Academy of Marketing Science.

Reddy, Allan C., John E. Oliver, C. P. Rao, and A. L. Addington (1984). "A Macro Behavioral Model of the Japanese Economic Miracle." *Akron Business and Economic Review* (Spring): 40–45.

Reich, Robert B. (1990). "Who Is Us?" *Harvard Business Review* 68 (January-February): 53–64.

Reis, Al, and Jack Trout (1986). *Positioning: The Battle for Your Mind,* rev. ed. New York: McGraw-Hill.

Rieker, W. S. (1977). *Quality Control Circles Study Guide.* Saratoga, Calif.: Internorth.

Schiffman, Leon G., and Leslie Lazar Kanuk (1983). *Consumer Behavior,* 2nd ed. Englewood Cliffs, N.J.: Prentice-Hall.

Schmenner, Roger W., and Randall L. Cook (1985). "Explaining Productivity Differences in North Carolina Factories." *Journal of Operations Management* 8 (July-August): 273–289.

Schonberger, R. J. (1992). *Japanese Manufacturing Techniques: Nine Hidden Lessons in Simplicity.* New York: Free Press.

Schuller, Robert H., and Paul David Dunn (1985). *The Power of Being Debt Free.* New York: Thomas Nelson.

Scott, Bruce R. (1989). "Competitiveness: Self-Help for a Worsening Problem." *Harvard Business Review* 67 (July-August): 115–121.

Shanklin, William L. (1989). *Six Timeless Marketing Blunders.* Lexington, Mass.: Lexington Books.

Shingo, S. (1982). *The Toyota Production System.* Tokyo: Japan Management Association.

Silbaugh, Kate (1988). "Automating Sales." *Systems 3X World* 16 (November): 33–39.

Starr, Martin K. (1988). *Global Competitiveness: Getting the U.S. Back on Track.* New York: W. W. Norton.

Steiner, George A. (1979). *Strategic Planning*. New York: Free Press.

Szymanski, David M., Sundar G. Bhardwaj, and P. Rajan Varadarajan (1993). "An Analysis of the Market Share–Profitability Relationship." *Journal of Marketing* 57 (July): 1–18.

Taguchi, Genichi, and Don Clausing (1990). "Robust Quality." *Harvard Business Review* 68 (January-February): 65–75.

Thurow, Lester (1993). *Head to Head: The Coming Economic Battle among Japan, Europe, and America*. New York: Warner Books.

Tull, Donald S., and Lynn R. Kahle (1990). *Marketing Management*. New York: Macmillan.

U.S. Foreign Trade Highlights 1988. Washington, D.C.: Office of Trade and Investment Analysis, International Trade Administration, U.S. Department of Commerce.

U.S. Foreign Trade Highlights 1992. Washington, D.C.: Office of Trade and Investment Analysis, International Trade Administration, U.S. Department of Commerce.

Venkataraman, V. K. (1981). "The Price-Quality Relationship in an Experimental Setting." *Journal of Advertising Research* 21 (August): 49–52.

Waldman, Raymond J. (1986). *Managed Trade*. Cambridge, Mass.: Ballinger.

Walton, Sam M. (1986). *Annual Report Given at Wal-Mart Annual Stockholders' Meeting*. Fayetteville, Ark.: Wal-Mart.

Weber, William P. (1988). "Manufacturing as a Competitive Strategy." In Furino, Antonio, ed., *Cooperation and Competition in Global Economy: Issues and Strategies*. Cambridge, Mass.: Ballinger, pp. 15–54.

Whirlpool Corporation (1983). *The Whirlpool Report on Consumers in Eighties: America's Search for Quality*. Benton Harbor, Mich.: The Corporation.

Zeithaml, Valerie A. (1988). "Consumer Perceptions of Price, Quality, and Value: A Means-End Model and Synthesis of Evidence." *Journal of Marketing* 52 (July): 2–22.

Zeithaml Valerie A., A. Parasuraman, and Leonard L. Berry (1990). *Delivering Quality Service*. New York: Free Press.

Additional Readings

Adams, Walter, and James W. Brock (1986). *The Bigness Complex.* New York: Pantheon.

Anderson, Gary M. (1987). "U.S. Federal Deficit and National Debt: A Political and Economic History." In Tollison, Robert D., ed., *Deficits.* New York: Basil Blackwell, pp. 9–46.

Arnesen, Peter J., ed. (1987). *The Japanese Competition: Phase 2.* Ann Arbor, Mich.: University of Michigan, Center for Japanese Studies.

Atlanta Constitution (1989). "Consumer Trends Change Convenience over Loyalty." 24 September, p. R-2.

Banker-UK (1987). "Japanese Banks Undercut a Bigger Slice." March, pp. 50–51.

Bessom, R. M. (1973). "Unique Aspects of Marketing Services." *Arizona Business* 20 (November): 8–15.

Brown, Paul B. (1989). "When Quality Isn't Everything." *Inc.* June, pp. 119–120.

Certon, Marvin, Alicia Pagano, and Otis Port (1985). *The Future of American Business: The U.S. in World Competition.* New York: McGraw-Hill.

Cravens, Donald W., Charles W. Holland, Charles W. Lamb, Jr., and William C. Montcrief III (1988). "Marketing's Role in Product and Service Quality." *Industrial Marketing Management* 17 (November): 285–304.

Damanpur, Faramarz (1988). "The Foreign Banking Invasion." *Bankers Monthly,* 16 May.

Engholm, Christopher (1991). *When Business East Meets Business West: The Guide to Practice and Protocol in the Pacific Rim.* New York: John Wiley.

Feenstra, Robert C., ed. (1989). *Trade Policies for International Competitiveness.* Chicago: University of Chicago Press.

Friedman, Milton, and Rose Friedman (1980). *Free to Choose.* New York: Avon Books.

Fudd, Leonard M. (1988). *Monitoring the Competition.* New York: John Wiley.

Garvin, David A. (1987). "Competing on the Eight Dimensions of Quality." *Harvard Business Review* 65 (November-December): 101–109.

——. (1984). "Product Quality: An Important Strategic Weapon." *Business Horizons* 27 (March-April): 40–43.

Iacocca, Lee, and Sonny Klenfield (1988). *Talking Straight.* New York: Bantam Books.

Ishihara, Shintaro (1991). *The Japan That Can Say No.* New York: Simon & Schuster.

Ishikawa, Kaoru (1985). *What Is Total Quality Control? The Japanese Way.* Englewood Cliffs, N.J.: Prentice-Hall.

Jacobson, Robert, and David A. Aaker (1987). "The Strategic Role of Product Quality." *Journal of Marketing* 51 (October): 31–44.

Juran, Joseph M. (1981). "Product Quality: A Prescription for the West, Part II: Upper-Management Leadership and Employee Relations." *Management Review* (July): 61.

——. (1988). *Juran on Planning for Quality.* New York: Free Press.

——. (1993). "Made in U.S.A.: A Renaissance in Quality." *Harvard Business Review* 71 (July-August): 42–50.

Krantz, K. Theodore (1989). "How Velcro Got Hooked on Quality." *Harvard Business Review* 67 (September-October): 34–40.

Lichenstein, Donald R., and Scot Burton (1989). "The Relationship between Perceived and Objective Price-Quality." *Journal of Marketing Research* 26 (November): 429–443.

McClenahen, J. S. (1992). "North America's New Shape." *Industry Week*, September 21, pp. 25–34.

McGaughey, W. (1992). *A U.S.–Mexico–Canada Free Trade Agreement: Do We Just Say No?* Minneapolis: Thistlerose.

McMahon, P. J. (1992). "U.S. Governors Hail NAFTA." *World Business Review* (November/December): 15–28.

Mitroff, Ian I., Susan A. Mohrman, and Geoffrey Little (1987). *Business NOT as Usual: Rethinking Our Individual, Corporate, and Industrial Strategies for Global Competition.* San Francisco: Jossey-Bass.

Moskal, B. S. (1993). "NAFTA: A Time-Release Capsule for Shippers." *Industry Week*, April 5, pp. 53–56.

Nakazawa, Kazuo (1989). "Containing Japan Is Not the Answer." *The Japan Times Weekly*, overseas edition, 23 September, p. 8.

NeVaer, Louis E. V., and Steven A. Deck (1989). *The Protectionist Threat to Corporate America: The U.S. Trade Deficit and Management Responses.* New York: Quorum.

Ouchi, William (1982). *Theory Z: How American Business Can Meet the Japanese Challenge.* Reading, Mass.: Warner Communications.

Parasuraman, A., Valerie A. Zeithaml, and Leonard L. Berry (1988). "SERVQUAL: A Multiple-Item Scale for Measuring Customer Perceptions of Service Quality." *Journal of Retailing* 64 (Spring): 12–40.

Peters, Tom, and Robert H. Waterman, Jr. (1982). *In Search of Excellence.* New York: Warner Books.

Philips, L. W., D. R. Chang, and Robert D. Buzzell (1983). "Product Quality, Cost Position, and Business Performance: A Test of Some Key Hypotheses." *Journal of Marketing* 47 (Spring): 26–43.

Quelch, John A., Robert D. Buzzell, and Eric R. Salama (1991). *The Marketing Challenge of EC 1992.* Reading, Mass.: Addison-Wesley.

Rabino, Samuel, and Elva Ellen Hubbard (1984). "The Race of American and Japanese Personal Computer Manufacturers for Dominance of the U.S. Market." *Columbia Journal of World Business* 19 (Fall): 18–31.

Rao, Akshay R., and Kent B. Monroe (1989). "The Effect of Price, Brand Name, and Store Name on Buyers' Perceptions of Product Quality: An Integrative Review." *Journal of Marketing Research* 26 (August): 351–357.

Reddy, Jack, and Abe Berger (1983). "Three Essentials of Product Quality." *Harvard Business Review* 61 (July-August): 153–159.

Richardson, Peter R. (1988). *Cost Containment: The Ultimate Advantage*. New York: Free Press.

Ryan, Edward, Jr. (1989). "Has the Marketing Concept Returned to the United States?" *Journal of Business and Industrial Marketing* (Summer-Fall): 61–63.

Shetty, Y. K. (1987). "Product Quality and Competitive Strategy." *Business Horizons* 30 (May-June): 46–52.

Skrentny, Roger (1987). "Japan Takes Detroit for a Ride." *Marketing Communications*, April, pp. 70–76, 86.

Sobel, Robert (1979). *IBM vs. Japan—The Struggle for the Future*. New York: Stein and Day.

Takeuchi, Hirotaka, and John A. Quelch (1983). "Quality Is More Than Making a Good Product." *Harvard Business Review* 61 (July-August): 139–145.

Taylor, Alex III (1989). "Here Comes Japan's New Luxury Car." *Fortune*, August, pp. 62–66

Thomas, Robert J. (1989). "Patent Infringement of Innovations by Foreign Competitors: The Role of the U.S. International Trade Commission." *Journal of Marketing* 53 (October): 63–75.

Time (1989). "Is, Government Dead?" 23 October, pp. 28–32.

U.S. Department of Commerce, International Trade Administration (1993). "The Beginning of a New Era." April 24.

U.S. General Accounting Office (1992). "North American Free Trade Agreement: U.S.–Mexican-Trade and Investment Data." September 25.

Viner, Aron (1988). *The Emerging Power of Japanese Money*. Homewood, Ill.: Dow Jones-Irwin.

Vogel, Ezra F. (1985). *Comeback—Case by Case: Building the Resurgence of American Business*. New York: Simon & Schuster.

Whicker, Marcia Lynn, and Raymond A. Moore (1988). *Making America Competitive: Policies for Global Future*. New York: Praeger.

Author Index

Subject Index

ABOUT THE AUTHOR

ALLAN C. REDDY is Professor of Marketing at Valdosta State University where he has been teaching marketing courses since 1980. Before that, he taught at Tennessee Technological University. He has written more than 50 articles published in various business journals and is a consultant to Johnson Wax Associates on international licensing. He also has consulting experience in health care. Dr. Reddy has published in the *Journal of Health Care Marketing* and co-authored *Marketing's Role in Economic Development* with David Campbell (Quorum, 1994).

ISBN 0-89930-893-7

HARDCOVER BAR CODE